Assemblies

Feasts Mary and the Saints

Volume 2

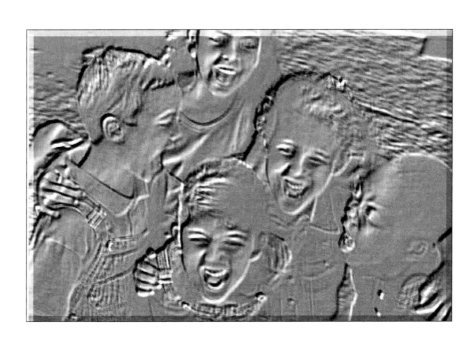

Jude Groden RSM

Christopher O'Donnell O.CARM

FOREWORD BY
Lord David Alton

MCCRIMMONS
Great Wakering, Essex, England

*The images used inside this book are taken from two CD volumes
and are available from the publishers.*

Signs, Symbols & Saints – Vol.1   Ref: SSSCD
Religious Clip Art on CD – Omnibus Edition   Ref: COCDP

First published in 2000 by
MCCRIMMON PUBLISHING CO. LTD.
10-12 High Street, Great Wakering, Essex SS3 0EQ
Telephone 01702–218956
Fax 01702–216082
Email: mccrimmons@dial.pipex.com
Web site: www.mccrimmons.co.uk

ISBN 0 85597 617 9 (Assemblies Vol.2 – Feasts Mary and the Saints)
ISBN 0 85597 615 2 (Assemblies Vol.1 – for liturgical seasons & school occasions)

Illustrations by The Benedictine Nuns of Turvey Abbey

Cover design and page layout: Nick Snode
Typeset in Revival 12pt roman and Frutiger 11/13pt roman
Printed by Polestar Wheatons Ltd, Exeter

Contents

Contents

Foreword

A worried parent asked their daughter how she had got on in her examinations. 'Music' came the reply, "failed the theory, passed the practice; chemistry, failed the theory, passed the practice; religious education, passed the theory, failed the practice."
Many of us know the theory of the Catholic faith all too well but, like the young woman, we fail in the practice.
Religious assemblies are a place where theory and practice meet; a time when belief and action converge.

When assemblies become rituals and fail to inspire they can do more harm than good. Children are pretty intuitive and it's not long before they realise that the disconsolate teacher leading them mindlessly through yet another verse of "Lord of the Dance" doesn't believe a word of it. And they rapidly see through religion devoid of reverence or relevance to the world in which they live.

St Augustine said that we should pray as if the entire outcome depends upon God, and work as if the entire outcome depends upon us. This means praying and working in a focused way.

Two hundred years ago William Wilberforce and his Christian friends in politics spent forty years of their lives in dedicated prayer and action. They were successful in abolishing slavery – the odious belief that it was a man's right to own another man as their slave, merely because of the colour of their skin.

Two hundred years earlier St Thomas More, the former Lord Chancellor and Speaker of the House of Commons, was executed for opposing laws which he knew to be wrong. He said he was "the King's good servant but God's first." He knew that faith combined with action can cost you everything – even your life.

At the time of writing this foreword a young English Catholic, James Mawdsley, is locked up in a tiny prison cell in Burma. Jailed for 17 years by the Burmese military regime, he has been imprisoned because his faith led him to peacefully demonstrate against an unjust regime. He is what Pope John Paul has called young people to be: "signs of contradiction."

Other British and Irish Catholics have been at the forefront of campaigns to end the massive burdens of Third World debt, the sale of arms to countries such as Indonesia, the fight to free East Timor, and campaigns closer to home against eugenics, abortion, euthanasia, genetic engineering, embryo experimentation and human cloning. Through their support for the work of agencies such as Life, Cafod, the Jubilee Campaign and the hospice movement they are passing the practice as well as the theory.

In all these ways young people are demonstrating how faith and action walk hand in hand. they are being true to the tradition of Thomas More and William Wilberforce. They are doing what Jesus told us to do when He said "Be salt and light" in the wold. Their formation takes place in our homes, in their parishes, and in their schools.

We owe it to them to pass on a love of their faith and understanding of the Catholic tradition. Martin Luther King once said that religious belief is destroyed when we make it dry as dust. Here is a resource which is full of life and full of ideas.

David Alton
Professor the Lord Alton of Liverpool
Crossbench member of the House of Lords

Introduction

School Worship

The School Assembly offers an opportunity and a challenge. For some schools it is a legal demand, one indeed open to many interpretations within the Education Reform Act (1988), which specifies that school worship is to be both religious and educational. Whilst few perhaps will doubt the potential of school assemblies and worship, many practical problems emerge from day to day. There are issues of content and approach to such worship; not all in the school will see it the same way, value it similarly, or engage in it with the same commitment. There are difficulties about guiding such worship and the ages and aptitudes of those participating. There is surely a problem from the very regularity of school worship: few people can be continually creative; constant innovation may be detrimental to the religious and educational aims of worship; sameness can lead to a stultifying monotony.

There is surely no one approach to school worship. Even within a Christian or more particularly a Catholic ethos, there are very many legitimate ways of communal worship that answer the guidelines given by educational authorities. The present volume seeks to help schools with worship drawing on contemporary insights about spirituality and doctrines in a way that would be helpful in both a religious and an educational perspective. Other models of assembly will have their place too. This book of assemblies offer teachers an outline that may either be followed quite closely, or better still, used as a framework within mainly primary and lower secondary schools. Trial use of assemblies of the first volume in various schools showed that the approach and content were helpful to hard-pressed teachers.

Aims of school worship

Even within the broad aims of school worship as religious and educational, there are many interpretations and possibilities. An earlier generation would perhaps have seen worship as self-justifying, something that the Christian would want to do, and which needs no further apology. Our age is more pragmatic and result conscious, and poses the question, what use is school worship? An immediate answer might be to say that an education that looks to the whole person cannot neglect a spiritual dimension of the individual and of the school itself. The frequently quoted DFE Circular 1/94, § 50 gives a number of aims that indicate possibilities of worship for the life of pupils and the school:

> "Collective worship in schools should aim...
>
> ❍ to provide the opportunity for pupils to worship God
> ❍ to consider spiritual and moral issues
> ❍ to explore their own beliefs
> ❍ to encourage participation and response whether through active involvement in the presentation of worship or through listening to and joining in the worship offered
> ❍ to develop community spirit
> ❍ to promote a common ethos and shared values
> ❍ to reinforce positive attitudes."

These aims can be seen to reflect an important teaching of the Second Vatican Council, "One of the gravest errors of our time is the dichotomy between the faith which many profess and their day-to-day conduct." (*Church in the Modern World*, GS 43)
One way of avoiding such a division between faith and daily life is to seek to integrate life and worship. Our daily lives lead into worship; our worship must flow over into our lives. It is helped when one can find a religious perspective for the concerns of daily life, and show that the affairs of daily life are not alien to religion and worship. The assemblies in this volume attempt just such integration and in so doing would wish to work for the aims in the DEF Circular.

The Saints in our Lives

In one of the early creeds, the so-called "Apostles' Creed," we profess our faith in "the Communion of Saints." This phrase is well explained in the *Catechism of the Catholic Church* (arts. 946–959). The creed invites us to broaden our minds to the great mystery of the family of God. The word "Communion" has the idea of sharing or fellowship. When we think of the Communion of Saints, we are in fact thinking about a sharing in holy things, and a sharing between holy people (the Latin and Greek *sanctorum/tôn hagiôn* can be personal or neuter signifying either persons or things). The holy things refer to the sacraments, prayers and all the good deeds and holiness of God's people living and dead. The "holy persons" refer primarily to all the saints in heaven, but also all of God's holy people on earth and those being healed in purgatory.

Canonisation

When we use the word "saints" we naturally think of those who have been canonised. Canonisation is an act of the pope, which solemnly proclaims that a person practised heroic virtue and lived in fidelity to God's grace (*Catechism of the Catholic Church*, art. 828). The first person to be thus canonised was St. Ulrich of Augsburg, whom Pope John XV raised to the altar in 993. The word "canonisation" originally meant that the person was mentioned in the Eucharistic Prayer (the "Canon") after Mary and the apostles. Before that people were canonised by what was called the voice of the people: the Church as a whole or in an area recognised the holiness of some man or woman.

When the Church canonises persons, they are given to us as models (*Catechism of the Catholic Church*, arts. 1717, 2030). They show us new ways in which the gospel can be lived. They invite us to think of the great work of the Holy Spirit in the Church. We can also see the saints as our friends, people we can turn to in our needs. We can always ask the saints to pray for us (*Catechism of the Catholic Church*, art. 956). It has long been the custom to give a saint's name at baptism or confirmation, somebody to whom we can look for inspiration and help (*Catechism of the Catholic Church*, 2156).

Holiness is for all

The Second Vatican Council insisted that not only the "official" saints, but all of us are called to be holy (*Catechism of the Catholic Church* art. 2013–2016; see Vatican II *Church*, art. 40). Holiness, which means genuine and generous love for God and for others, is to be sought in the deeds of everyday living, "among the pots and pans", as the great St. Teresa of Avila liked to say. The other Teresa, St. Thérèse of Lisieux, the Little Flower, gave us a doctrine of "the Little Way" to holiness, which was to do ordinary things extraordinarily well, offering them to God, and loving others.

The Saints and assemblies

This volume looks to some key feasts of Christ, of Mary as well as the saints to show the Christian life lived to the full. It is not possible, nor desirable, to pray to a very large number of saints on a regular basis. But by having assemblies which place before the school, the Virgin Mary, various saints and the mysteries of Christ in this volume as well as in the first companion volume, we seek to broaden the vision of what it is to be a Christian and to show different possibilities of meeting our friends in the Communion of Saints.

The reader's attention is drawn to the explanatory pages in the first volume, which outline the significant elements of the assemblies (see *Assemblies* – Volume One pp. 7–11). A few points may be made about this second volume.

Features of school assemblies

The structure and elements of the school assemblies in this work stress some important features of school worship and might be seen as answering the aims mentioned earlier.

1 Entrance music (tape or CD)

It is suggested that when pupils come to assembly that there be some suitable background music being played. This will help to set the atmosphere for the worship, which is to follow. It helps the pupils to realise that in some way the worship time is special, set apart from the other activities of the school day. Though God is everywhere present in supporting creation, there is a special presence of Christ in the reading of scripture and in the prayer and singing of those who gather in his name (see Vatican II, *Liturgy*, SC 7).

2 Introduction

There is a short overview of the saints' lives, locating them in time and place. In many cases these saints are invoked as patrons by groups of people or countries, etc.

3 Focus or symbol

Reflects an aspect of the saint's life. It would seem important to have the saint's name on an overhead, so that all may be able to spell and pronounce the saint's name. The symbol given usually on the top right-hand corner of each assembly in this book might be photocopied and used on an overhead.

The use of a focus or symbol helps to bring out the theme of the celebration. It is a centre of attention. The focus or symbol is yet another way in which school worship is a transfer to sacred time or space, yet within the practicalities of ordinary life.

Various suggestions are made that schools will wish to modify. For special occasions more attention can be given to providing a symbol or focus, but for regular school worship it will not be possible to provide a stimulating symbol for every day.

A question can arise about explaining symbols. Symbols are generally open, and can be entered into at various levels: a flag or poster will move people differently. Though it is sometimes helpful to draw people's attention to a symbol, detailed explanations can kill a symbol. The explanation restricts the meaning that others will take from it; the power of the symbol is cut off by words. People can share in a symbol without understanding it or how it operates. Indeed it would be better to say that symbols do not so much explain as open up meaning. A picture of a dove on an overhead can allow people to enter into the quiet of the dove, its freedom, its lightness, and its simple beauty. Such feelings – and symbols operate primarily at the level of feeling – could be cut off by telling the pupils too much about doves.

One cannot be absolute in this matter. Younger pupils can be helped to enter into the world of symbols, in which anyway they are already operating. But in general for older pupils, a good symbol does not need too much explanation. We draw attention to it and let it speak to the individual.

4 Sign of the Cross

Catholic prayer usually begins with the Sign of the Cross, "In the name of the Father and of the Son and of the Holy Spirit. Amen." This invocation is an entering into prayer. The brief introduction provides a transition from the Introduction to actual prayer.

5 Hymn or song

Opinions will vary about the best place for hymns. If they are placed at the very beginning pupils may not be sufficiently attentive or alert, and the meaning can be lost. The hymn is a way in which pupils can actively take part in the worship of the assembly. At times a taped hymn may be used, especially when a hymn or song is not yet familiar, but in general it would seem to be better to have the pupils sing rather than to listen to a song. There are two extremes to be avoided: over frequent use of the same hymn can lead to monotony in hymns, and people grow tired even of favourite ones. But on the other hand a school repertoire can only be built up slowly. The hymns given for the assemblies in this book are only examples of what might be appropriate for a particular celebration.

6 Reading

The reading is generally chosen from scripture and is very often the text chosen by the Church for the Mass of the saint. This choice has a double thrust. The scripture points to some important feature of the saint's life; the saint's life is in some ways a commentary on the practical meaning of the biblical text.

Care needs to be taken that the reading does lead to the double focus of school worship, namely being religious and educational. In the last few decades the Catholic Church has given ever-increasing attention to scripture as the source of its life and its worship. In the scriptures we hear God's word that lifts us up, instructs us, corrects us, trains us in holiness (see 2 Tim 3:16-17).

Moreover the reading is yet another example of how the life of the school radiates outwards and upwards. The scripture draws our attention to the need to be serving and loving in our school, family and society; it also reminds us of God's loving providence which surrounds us and continually leads us to God and the great mysteries.

7 Comment on reading

As in the case of symbols we have to avoid being too clear-cut in explanations of the readings. But they are not self-evident and we can always be enriched by the insights of another into a passage, even one that we think we already thoroughly know. The living faith of teachers who meet with God's word and then share in a simple way what this word means to them is a powerful witness. The comments in this book are merely suggestive about ways in which the scripture text can be integrated into the act of the worship, and the lives of the pupils and teachers.

8 Response to the reading

There are many possibilities. The teacher is invited to be particularly creative here. The suggested responses merely indicate some possible direction arising from the readings and the life of the saint. Interactive responses are encouraged.

9 Prayers

Prayers seek to open the minds of the school community to the wider needs of the Church and of the world. At the same time these prayers are a special time for each one, teachers and pupils, to come before God in confidence with their needs. The suggested prayers usually continue the themes of the readings or features of the life of the saint. In this way it is hoped that there is in the assembly an actual teaching on how to pray, and the generous range that should characterise Christian prayer.

10 Thought-Word-Phrase for the Day

The period of worship is a highpoint of the day. It cannot remain isolated, and should carry over into the rest of the day. One way to help this process is the selection of a thought, word or phrase that is given to the assembly at the end that sums up or focuses what has been celebrated. One should not underestimate the possibilities of such a phrase. We are all familiar with the power of advertising and the way in which its subliminal messages fashion our attitudes towards particular products or services. We are the same creatures of mind and body that are influenced by secular advertising as well also by Christian thoughts. The worship with its readings, symbols, prayers and ideas will gradually transform us. The use of a Thought-Word-Phrase for the day is one way in which the school communicates values. The ones given in this volume are of course only suggestions. Were other teachers to refer occasionally to the Thought-Word-Phrase at some later time, then there would be possibilities for still deeper integration of worship and life.

11 Blessing

In the past blessings were almost exclusively associated with ordained ministers, and indeed some blessings are still their special competence. But the rediscovery of Celtic spirituality in these islands has alerted us to a profound theme in Christian life, as seen especially by the Celtic peoples in our society. A very common greeting in Celtic languages such as Welsh, Scots Gaelic and Irish was a blessing, "God bless all here," "God bless the work," "Praise God for a beautiful day."

Blessing in scripture had a double meaning. It was something that we received from God; it is a bringing before God of people, circumstances and things. Such blessings are often expressed as a wish or a prayer directed to God. The blessings in this volume are again only indicative of the sort of conclusion that the worship might have.

Some biblical blessings are used frequently to make them familiar, such as Numbers 6:24-26 and 2 Corinthians 13:13. These are used extensively by various Christian bodies as blessings, and in Catholic worship the latter is used as a liturgical greeting.

From a liturgical point of view one might state that in using these blessings the leader of the assembly and all present could make the sign of the Cross on themselves. It is not appropriate for one who is not a deacon or priest to impose hands over the assembly or to make the sign of the Cross over them, as an official act of blessing during liturgical worship.

12 Concluding song or music

The concluding music may be a hymn sung by all, it may also be music already recorded. Its aim is to create a bridge of transition back to other school realities.

Key for hymnbooks

CFE	=	Celebration Hymnal for Everyone
O&N	=	Hymns Old & New
YOC	=	A Year of Celebration
CH	=	The Complete Celebration Hymnal with New Songs of Celebration
GW	=	Great Week

Mary Mother of God

1 Entrance music (tape or CD) Choose a suitable piece of music

2 Introduction

Mary was God's chosen way for the Son to come into the world. She was his mother, the God-bearer. On behalf of us all she said a complete "yes" to God's plan to save us. She is the first member of the Church. Mary is the model of all mothers and of all who want to come close to Jesus who is our Life. We begin the New Year under her guidance and protection.

3 Focus or symbol

- Crib
- Poster with Mary and the child Jesus
- Overhead/caption: *"Mary Mother of God."*

4 Sign of the Cross

The Cross is a reminder of God's great love for us in sending Jesus into the world that we might have life. Together with Mary, our Mother, we marvel at this love and begin, "In the name of the Father and of the Son and of the Holy Spirit."

5 Hymn or song

CFE		O&N
51	As we come before you	-
-	When Mary listened to God's word	611
YOC		
45	Hail Mary	-

 6 Reading *Luke 2:16–20 (paraphrased)*

The shepherds hurried off and found Mary and Joseph and saw the baby lying in the manger. When the shepherds saw him, they told them what the angel had said about the child. All who heard it were amazed at what the angel said. Mary remembered all these things and thought deeply about them. The shepherds went back singing praises to God for all they had heard and seen.

7 Comment on reading

We cannot take in deep things at a glance or in a moment. The crib is very simple, but we can look at it for a long time, before we hear its deep message. The God who created all the galaxies, all the stars, the whole world, this God became a little baby and lay on the floor in a stable, in a little hollowed out space, where the animals' food was placed, a manger. What a wonder! What love! And it took Mary a long time to take it all in. We need time too.

8 Response to reading

Think of how much we owe to our own mothers. They have cared for us, they gave us life. What greater gift could they have given us? Candles are lit by class representatives to express our thanks to God for Mary, and our thanks too, for our own mothers.

9 Prayers

At the beginning of this New Year we pray with Mary our Mother.

[a]	That all Christians may come closer to Jesus this year.
Response:	**Mother of God, pray for us.**
[b]	That all who live in darkness may find love.
Response:	**Mother of God, pray for us.**
[c]	That all mothers, especially those having difficulties, may be blessed by God and by their family.
Response:	**Mother of God, pray for us.**
[d]	That all peoples may live in peace.
Response:	**Mother of God, pray for us.**
[e]	That we will be more loving, caring and thankful in our families.
Response:	**Mother of God, pray for us.**
[f]	[other prayers]
Response:	**Mother of God, pray for us.**
[g]	Our Father [perhaps sung]

10 Thought–Word–Phrase for the day

Jesus, show me your Mother; Mary, show me your Son

Prayer ascribed to St. Ignatius

11 Blessing

May our loving God bless us as we strive to follow Jesus and listen to him. Amen.

12 Concluding song or music

CFE		O&N
643	Silent Night	477

The Epiphany

1 Entrance music (tape or CD) Choose a suitable piece of music

2 Introduction

The word "Epiphany" means "showing." From the very early centuries of the Church three great showings or manifestations of Jesus were commemorated: he was shown to the wise men, who represented all the peoples of the earth; he was shown to his disciples when he changed wine into water (John 2); he was shown to the Jewish people at his baptism. As the ancient hymn says:

> "Manifested by the star
> To the sages from afar…
> Manifest at Jordan's stream,
> Prophet, priest and king
>   supreme,
> And at Cana wedding guest
> In they Godhead manifest."

More particularly today we remember the three wise men, traditionally called, Melchior, Balthasar and Casper. They brought three gifts each with a deep meaning:

- – Gold to tell us that Jesus was king.
- – Incense to remind us that Jesus is the Son of God.
- – Myrrh to tell us about his passion and death.

3 Focus

- – A large star
- – Crib with three wise men
- – Three wrapped gifts

4 Sign of the Cross

The Cross is God's greatest gift to us, for by it we have been saved, and so we begin "In the name of the Father and of the Son and of the Holy Spirit."

5 Hymn or song

CFE		O&N
788	We three kings	601
692	The first Nowell	523

 6 Reading   *Matthew 2:1-12*
(paraphrased)

Soon after Jesus was born three wise men came to Jerusalem. A bright star had led them from their own country, and they knew that a king had been born. The corrupt King Herod did not like the idea of another king as a rival so he planned to kill the child Jesus. He told them that the Jewish people were expecting a great King or Messiah to be born in Bethlehem. They went and found Mary and Joseph. They worshipped him and gave their gifts of gold, incense and myrrh. Then they went back to their own country, avoiding Herod and his city Jerusalem.

7 Comment on reading

The wise men travelled hundreds of miles through the desert to find Jesus. We can imagine that they were often down and doubting, but they continued to follow the star. We too follow the same star, which will lead us to Jesus. We learn this way from the bible, from the Church, from teachers and from our parents.

8 Response to reading

A candle is lit and placed beside the star.
All sing the verse from the Adeste hymn
("*Come all ye faithful*")
    "O come let us adore him,
      O come let us adore him,
      Christ the Lord." *(repeat several times)*
                             (CFE 520)

9 Prayers

We turn to Jesus our King and pray:

[a] That all who search for you will find you.
Response: **Show yourself to the world.**

[b] That the poor and needy may be helped.
Response: **Show yourself to the world.**

[c] That Governments and local authorities may care for all our people.
Response: **Show yourself to the world.**

[d] That those who have lost their way may find Jesus as their light.
Response: **Show yourself to the world.**

[e] That we may have courage to keep going when things are difficult.
Response: **Show yourself to the world.**

[f] [other prayers]
Response: **Show yourself to the world.**

[g] Our Father [perhaps sung]

10 Thought, word, phrase for the day

What gift can I offer Jesus today?

11 Blessing

May we like the wise men always seek Jesus and show him to others. Amen.

12 Concluding music or song

CFE		*O&N*
202	Go tell it on the mountain	187

St Anthony of Egypt

1 Entrance music (tape or CD) Choose a suitable piece of music

2 Introduction

There are two great saints called Anthony. We celebrate the feast of St. Anthony of Padua in June, today we think about St. Anthony who was born in Egypt about 251, and died about 356. As a young man he heard the words of the Gospel read at Mass, "Go sell what you have, give the money to the poor, and come follow me." He was struck later by the words of Jesus, "Do not be anxious about your life, what you are to eat." Anthony took these words with great seriousness. After providing for his only sister, he gave away everything and went into the desert. He was a holy man and people gathered around him asking to be guided in the ways of God. This was the beginning of the monastic or religious life, and Anthony was regarded as the first abbot.

Anthony is seen as the patron saint of basket makers, butchers and of domestic animals. His symbol is a bell.

3 Focus or symbol

- Bell or basket
- Overhead/caption/poster with words: *"Go sell what you have, give the money to the poor and follow me."*

4 Sign of the Cross

Early writers and artists show us Anthony with a simple Cross, which he used whenever he was in need, and so we begin, "In the name of the Father and of the Son and of the Holy Spirit."

5 Hymn or song

CFE		O&N
175	Follow me, follow me	145

6 Reading   *Matthew 19:21*

Jesus said, "If you want to be perfect, go and sell all you have and give the money to the poor, and you will have riches in heaven; then come and follow me."

7 Comment on reading

Anthony received a special call from Jesus, and he gave up everything. He became a great saint and leader of the Christian people right down to our own day. The most important thing we learn from Anthony is not so much that he gave up all his money, but that he decided to follow Jesus with generosity. We can all do that. But at the same time it is vital that we do not see money as the biggest thing in life. Religion, love, friendship, health and many other things are more important than being rich.

8 Response to reading

Could you give even a little money to those in greater need than yourselves? A box for (specify charity) will be left for you to put something in today or tomorrow.

9 Prayers

We pray that like Anthony of Egypt we too may hear the words of Jesus and be generous.

[a]   That all who are in need or are being badly treated will receive help.
Response: **Lord, help me to be generous.**

[b]   That all who hear the call of Jesus in their lives may have the courage to do so.
Response: **Lord, help me to be generous.**

[c]   That all men and women who follow in the footsteps of Anthony as monks and hermits may be truly holy.
Response: **Lord, help me to be generous.**

[d]   That all in Anthony's homeland of Egypt and the Middle East may find peace.
Response: **Lord, help me to be generous.**

[e]   That we may not have excessive worries about money.
Response: **Lord, help me to be generous.**

[f]   [other prayers]
Response: **Lord, help me to be generous.**

[g]   Our Father [perhaps sung]

10 Thought-Word-Phrase for the day

Generosity is beautiful

11 Blessing

May we be open to God's words,
Receive them with love,
And live them with generosity.
    Amen.

12 Concluding song or music

CFE		O&N
148	Do not worry about what to eat	123

St Francis de Sales

1 Entrance music (tape or CD) Choose a suitable piece of music

2 Introduction

There are several great saints with the name Francis. Today we honour a French saint, Francis born at Chateau de Sales in 1567. He was a great scholar, and his family wanted him to enter government, but he chose rather to be a priest. He was later bishop of Geneva. His life was marked by love, by gentleness and by love for the Church. He is known for his great insistence that everybody is called to be holy. A favourite saying of his was that "more flies are attracted by a spoonful of honey than by a barrel full of vinegar." That is, we draw people by kindness.

He is the patron saint of Catholic writers and of journalists.

3 Focus or symbol

- A Catholic paper
- Jar of honey
- Caption: Drawing by kindness

4 Sign of the Cross

St. Francis was drawn always by the love, which he discovered in the Cross of Christ, and so we begin, "In the name of the Father and of the Son and of the Holy Spirit."

5 Hymn or song

CFE		O&N
268	How lovely on the mountains	224

6 Reading *John 15:12–14.16*

Jesus said, "my commandment is this: love one another, just as I have loved you. The greatest love a person can have for his friends is to give his life for them. And you are my friends if you do what I command you. You did not choose me; I chose you and appointed you to go and bear fruit, the kind of fruit that endures. And so the Father will give you whatever you ask in my name.

7 Comment on reading

We do not often use the word "holy." We think of it as something that is special and for remarkable saints only. Francis used another word, "devout" or "good" and said that we are all called to a good life, that is a holy life. His way of being good was especially to reach out to those in need, particularly those who were troubled in their faith or were anxious.

8 Response to reading

Let these words of St. Francis echo within us: "I will comfort and help your poor by what I do as well as what I say. I will go against sin in myself and help others to do the same."

9 Prayers

When sinners came to Francis, they found in him all the tenderness of a father. He used to say to them, "God and I will help you." With St. Francis de Sales, we turn to the God of all tenderness.

[a]   That bishops, priests and deacons may show the love of God especially in the sacraments of Reconciliation and Eucharist.
Response: **Lord, help us to love tenderly.**

[b]   That the poor and all in distress will find help and light.
Response: **Lord, help us to love tenderly.**

[c]   That those who find faith difficult or who have lapsed may find the tenderness of God.
Response: **Lord, help us to love tenderly.**

[d]   That Catholic authors and journalists may always seek truth.
Response: **Lord, help us to love tenderly.**

[e]   That we may be generous in our love for others, especially those whom we find difficult.
Response: **Lord, help us to love tenderly.**

[f]   [other prayers]
Response: **Lord, help us to love tenderly.**

[g]   Our Father [perhaps sung]

10 Thought-Word-Phrase for the day

St. Francis used to say:

*"The measure of love,
is to love without measure."*

11 Blessing

May the God of love and
    tenderness bless us.
May he show us how to be good
    today.
May he help us to love without
    measure.
    Amen.

12 Concluding song or music

CFE		*O&N*
739	Though the mountains may fall	569

The Conversion of St. Paul

1 Entrance music (tape or CD) Choose a suitable piece of music

2 Introduction

Paul, or Saul as he was first called, was not always a saint. Earlier as a loyal and angry Jew he persecuted the Church, but Jesus loved him even so and brought about his conversion. He was then sent on a mission to tell people about Jesus. This is the time that we pray for the conversion of sinners and for Christian unity.

St. Paul is patron of missionary bishops.

3 Focus or symbol

- Bible open at the letters of St. Paul

  and/or

- Picture/slide of shipwreck or of Paul's conversion

4 Sign of the Cross

Paul constantly preached about the death of Jesus that saved us, and so we begin, "In the name of the Father and of the Son and of the Holy Spirit."

5 Hymn or song

CFE		O&N
383	Lord Jesus Christ (Living Lord)	-
or		
-	Lord Jesus, you have come to us	326

 6 Reading   *Acts 9:1–3 (paraphrased)*

Saul was coming near the city of Damascus, when suddenly a light from the sky flashed around him. He fell down and heard a voice saying, "Saul, Saul, why do you persecute me?" Saul asked, "who are you?" and the voice replied, "I am Jesus, whom you are persecuting." Paul got up from the ground, but he was now blind. They took him by the hand and brought him to Damascus.
After three days Jesus sent a prophet called Ananias to go and pray for Paul. He laid his hands on him, and called him "Brother Saul." His sight was restored and he was baptised.

7 Comment on reading

Jesus takes as done to himself what we do to others. Saul was persecuting the Christians, but Jesus said that this was to persecute himself. But Jesus still loved Saul and had planned that he would be a great preacher and saint. He called him from sin to light. Ananias was chosen to restore Saul. Ananias forgave Saul for the dreadful persecution of his friends, and he called Saul, "brother." The Good News of Christianity is that we can always turn to God and receive forgiveness.

8 Response to reading

A number of pupils come forward to light votive lamps or candles:

- For those preparing for the sacrament of baptism;
- For those preparing for the sacrament of reconciliation;
- For those preparing for confirmation;
- For all Christian people.

9 Prayers

We pray for all that bring light to those in darkness.

[a] For all who are blind to God's love and truth.
Response: **St. Paul, pray for us to God.**

[b] For all members of the Church that they may come together in unity.
Response: **St. Paul, pray for us to God.**

[c] For all who live in the darkness of sin.
Response: **St. Paul, pray for us to God.**

[d] For all who find it hard to forgive.
Response: **St. Paul, pray for us to God.**

[e] For all who are blind or visually handicapped, and for opticians and eye doctors.
Response: **St. Paul, pray for us to God.**

[f] [Other prayers]
Response: **St. Paul, pray for us to God.**

[g] Our Father [perhaps sung]

10 Thought-Word-Phrase for the day

To be people of good news, being Christ for others

11 Blessing   *2 Corinthians 13:13*

The grace of the Lord Jesus Christ, the love of God and the fellowship of the Holy Spirit be with us all.
Amen.

12 Concluding song or music

CFE		O&N
285	I, the Lord of sea and sky	712
or		
295	If God is with us	231

St Thomas Aquinas

1 Entrance music (tape or CD) Choose a suitable piece of music

2 Introduction

Thomas was born of the Aquino family in Italy about 1225. His family had many troubles: one brother was jailed and executed for political crimes. Thomas joined the Dominicans and went to study. He was very quiet and the other students looked down on him, calling him the "dumb ox". But he was soon to be known as the most brilliant theologian in France and Italy. He was overweight and bald and seems to have suffered from depression in later life. Because he was a great scholar and a saint, he is named as one of the thirty-three "doctors of the Church." He died in 1274.

St. Thomas Aquinas is patron of all in education, especially religious education.

3 Focus or symbol

- Bible and/or Catechism of the Catholic Church.

4 Sign of the Cross

Thomas Aquinas wrote that we cannot know deep truth unless we know about the Cross of Christ, and so we begin, "In the name of the Father and of the Son and of the Holy Spirit."

5 Hymn or song

CFE		O&N
572	Oh the word of my Lord	431
or		
-	Our God sent his Son	435
or		
GW		
28	There is no greater love	

6 Reading   *from the writings of Thomas Aquinas*

"The Cross of Jesus Christ provides an example of every virtue. If you are looking for an example of love, "Greater love has no one that to lay down life for one's friends." This is what Christ did on the Cross. If he gave up his life for us, it ought not to be a burden for us to put up with trouble for his sake. If you are looking for patience, you will find it in the highest form on the Cross. If you are looking for an example of humility, look at the Cross. There God willed to be judged by Pilate and to die. If you are looking for an example of obedience, look to him who was obedient to the Father."

7 Comment on reading

St. Thomas teaches us that it is more important to be good than to be clever. The Dominican motto "Truth" (Veritas) guided him in all his study, writing and preaching. We may not be as brainy as St. Thomas, but we are to use whatever gifts we have to serve and help others. At the same time we should not be surprised or too upset when others turn against us, or misunderstand us.

8 Response to reading

One of the pupils and one of the teachers go up and kiss the Bible to show respect for God's word that leads us into truth.

9 Prayers

We pray for all involved in study of religion and who teach it.

[a]   We pray for all teachers in the Church.
Response: **Lord lead us into truth.**

[b]   We pray for those who write about religious matters.
Response: **Lord lead us into truth.**

[c]   We pray for the bodies and individuals that are concerned with and help religious education in the diocese.
Response: **Lord lead us into truth.**

[d]   We pray for those who are studying to be priests.
Response: **Lord lead us into truth.**

[e]   We pray that we may be eager to learn more about our religion.
Response: **Lord lead us into truth.**

[f]   [other prayers]
Response: **Lord lead us into truth.**

[g]   Our Father [perhaps sung]

10 Thought-Word-Phrase for the day

St. Thomas's love for the Word of God – respect even for the book

11 Blessing/Prayer

The Lord bless us, and keep us from all evil, and bring us to everlasting life.

12 Concluding song or music

CFE		O&N
688	The Church's one foundation	518
or		
156	Faith of our fathers	130

St John Bosco

1 Entrance music (tape or CD) Choose a suitable piece of music

2 Introduction

St. John Bosco was an Italian saint born in 1815 of very poor parents. After becoming a priest he began looking after homeless boys. Eventually he gathered people around him to help: these became the Salesians looking after boys, and Daughters of Our Lady Help of Christians caring for girls. He set up clubs for youth where skills were taught. He managed to win over even the most difficult children with kindness and encouragement.

St. John Bosco is patron of youth organisations.

3 Focus or symbol

- Candle
- Overhead/poster with name of youth organisations in the area

4 Sign of the Cross

The Cross continually reminds us of God's love for all, especially those who are unloved. With love, therefore, we begin "In the name of the Father and of the Son and of the Holy Spirit."

5 Hymn or song

CFE		O&N
-	Sing a simple song	481
670	Suffer little children	-
YOC		
177	Father, see your children	-

 6 Reading   *Matthew 18:3.5*
(paraphrased)

Jesus told everybody "unless you change and become like children, you will never enter the kingdom of heaven. Anyone who welcomes a child in my name, welcomes me.

7 Comment on reading

When Jesus told everybody, grown ups as well as young people, that they must be like children, he was not suggesting that children are perfect, and that there are no difficult children. What he is saying is that just as children cannot manage on their own without adults, so we cannot manage without God. Again, children have to be taught, so also everybody needs to be taught by God. The saint of today, St. John Bosco invites us to think of children who are in special need. People who help such a child is seen by Jesus as loving himself.

8 Response to reading

St. John Bosco had a special gift of helping children who were down-and-out. Is there any pupil who seems unhappy that we could play with, encourage or even talk to?

9 Prayers

God loves and listens to his children, and so we pray.

[a]	For parents, carers, priests and teachers.
Response:	**We are God's children.**
[b]	For youth groups and clubs.
Response:	**We are God's children.**
[c]	For children in need.
Response:	**We are God's children.**
[d]	For UNICEF which works world-wide for children.
Response:	**We are God's children.**
[e]	For ourselves at this time.
Response:	**We are God's children.**
[f]	[other prayers]
Response:	**We are God's children.**
[g]	Our Father [perhaps sung]

10 Thought-Word-Phrase for the day

*Encourage some
young person today*

11 Blessing

May the blessing of our generous
God come upon us.
May we bring hope to those we
meet.
May we reach out to people in
need.
Amen.

12 Concluding song or music

CFE		O&N
106	Christ be beside me	79

St Brigid

1 Entrance music (tape or CD) Choose a suitable piece of music

2 Introduction

There are several saints called Brigit, Brigid, Bridget or Bride. Today we celebrate an Irish saint born about 450. She is said to have been baptised by St. Patrick. She looked after cows and later became one of the first nuns in Ireland. She was noted for miracles of healing even during her life.

She is patron of poets and dairy-workers.

3 Focus or symbol

- St. Brigid's Cross made from rushes or reeds
- Book of poetry or book on farming

4 Sign of the Cross

St. Brigid was known for teaching people in her area about Jesus and so we begin "In the name of the Father and of the Son and of the Holy Spirit."

5 Hymn or song

CFE		O&N
347	Lay your hands	-
399	Love is his word (esp. stanzas 5-7)	338

 ## 6 Reading
Luke 11:27–28
(paraphrased)

When a woman in a crowd praised the mother of Jesus, he said that Mary's true greatness lay in hearing and obeying the word of God.

7 Comment on reading

St. Brigid is known as "The Mary of the Gael" because in her life she showed the virtues of Mary, the Mother of God. It is good to pray to Mary, but we should also try to live like her as Brigid did. Jesus tells us that being like his Mother is quite simply by hearing and obeying the word of God.

8 Response to reading

Two pupils come forward with lighted candles to remind us how much we owe to poets and to those who work on farms.

9 Prayers

God is always faithful to us and so we pray.

| [a] | That we may see more clearly the virtues of Mary, Mother of God. |
| Response: | **Lord help us to obey your word.** |

| [b] | That the work of farmers may be blessed. |
| Response: | **Lord help us to obey your word.** |

| [c] | That poets will raise our minds to see the world more fully. |
| Response: | **Lord help us to obey your word.** |

| [d] | That women's rights may be respected everywhere. |
| Response: | **Lord help us to obey your word.** |

| [e] | That we may not be distracted from following the word of God. |
| Response: | **Lord help us to obey your word.** |

| [f] | [other prayers] |
| Response: | **Lord help us to obey your word.** |

| [g] | Our Father [perhaps sung] |

10 Thought-Word-Phrase for the day

Listen to God's word to us, today

11 Blessing

The grace of our Lord Jesus Christ, the love of God and the fellowship of the Holy Spirit be with us all.
Amen.

12 Concluding song or music

CFE		*O&N*
285	Here I am Lord	-
-	My God said to me, Follow	360
YOC		
129	One more step	-

Presentation of the Lord

1 Entrance music (tape or CD) Choose a suitable piece of music

2 Introduction

Today might be called the final feast of the Christmas season. It is also called Candlemas ("Mass of the Candles") because candles are blessed and can be carried in procession on this day. Candles remind us that Christ is proclaimed in the temple as the "Light of the World."

Forty days after his birth Jesus was brought to the Temple in Jerusalem. There were two ceremonies there: one was to present or offer the child to God. This represented the truth that all life belongs to God. Jesus, even though little more than a month old, was offered to God so that he might be a saviour.

The second ceremony was for Mary his mother; she gave thanks for the birth of her Son. At the temple two holy old people, the prophets Simeon and Anna, recognised Jesus as Light and Saviour of the world. This idea of Jesus being light is recalled today with the presence of candles.

3 Focus or symbol

- A number of candles with only one lighting
- Crib figures: Mary, Joseph

4 Sign of the Cross

Today's feast of the Presentation looks forward to our redemption. Jesus is Saviour. We proclaim his Cross as we say, "In the name of the Father and of the Son and of the Holy Spirit."

5 Hymn or song

CFE		O&N
388	Shine, Jesus shine	-
703	The light of Christ	529

 6 Reading *Luke 2:22–38 (paraphrased)*

Mary and Joseph took the child Jesus to Jerusalem to present him to the Lord. Since they were poor, they could only offer two pigeons to the Lord as a sacrifice. Simeon was a holy old man who had prayed that he would see the Saviour before he died. The Holy Spirit guided him to recognise the world's Saviour in the baby carried by two poor country-people, Mary and Joseph. Simeon gave thanks and said, "Now at last I am prepared to die, because I have seen the Saviour, he is the light for all peoples." A holy old widow, Anna, also gave thanks and told people about Jesus.

7 Comment

We all know what it is to be without light. We may wake up at night and everything seems strange. Or there may be a power-cut and we start falling over things. But a light shows us how to avoid things and how to find what we need. Jesus is that light. Without his light, we get lost, fall over things, fall into sin. His light guides us to do the right thing. We find his light especially in the Bible and in the teaching of the Church. And so often it is the poor, those who do not seem to count in society, that most quickly and fully recognise Jesus and tell others about him.

8 Response to reading

The figure of the baby Jesus is carried in and placed beside the focus figures of Mary and Joseph. A representative from each class lights a candle from the central candle.

During this time the Taizé chant "The light of Christ" or other hymn may be played. "The Light of Christ" (CFE 703 or O&N 529) could be sung again.

9 Prayers

We think today about the ways God has given us light.

[a]	We give thanks for the light and life we have received in our lives.
Response:	**Jesus, you are the light of the world.**

[b]	We express our gratitude to all who have brought light and love to our lives.
Response:	**Jesus, you are the light of the world.**

[c]	We think of those who feel that they are living in darkness.
Response:	**Jesus, you are the light of the world.**

[d]	We ask the Lord to bless all who provide light, especially the Electricity Companies, which light our homes, and the councils which light our streets.
Response:	**Jesus, you are the light of the world.**

[e]	We remember the dead and pray that they may have the light of Christ forever.
Response:	**Jesus, you are the light of the world.**

[f]	[other prayers]
Response:	**Jesus, you are the light of the world.**

[g]	Our Father [perhaps sung]

10 Thought-Word-Phrase for the day

*The wonder of having light.
Can I be light for someone today?*

11 Blessing

May the Lord bless you and take care of you.
May the Lord be kind and gracious to you.
May the Lord look with favour on you and
   give you peace.
Amen.

12 Concluding song or music

CFE		O&N
110	Christ is our king	84
or repeat		
703	The light of Christ	529

St Blaise

1 Entrance music (tape or CD) Choose a suitable piece of music

2 Introduction

St. Blaise lived in Armenia and died about 316. Very little is known about him except that he was Bishop of Sivas and put to death for being a Christian. It is said that when he was hiding from persecution people who knew of his holiness brought sick animals for his blessing. On one occasion he saved the life of a small boy who had a fish-bone stuck in his throat. The mother of this child afterwards kept bringing him food and candles. In some places people have their throats blessed on this day with two candles.

St. Blaise is the patron invoked for sore throats and for sick cattle.

3 Focus or symbol

- Two unlit candles
- A scarf

4 Sign of the Cross

The martyrs like Blaise laid down their lives for Christ who had died for them on the Cross, and so we begin "In the name of the Father and of the Son and of the Holy Spirit."

5 Hymn or song

CFE		O&N
347	Lay your hands gently on us	295

6 Reading

Mark 16:15–18
(paraphrased)

Jesus told his disciples to go out to the whole world preaching, baptising and healing. He promised that when believers place their hands on sick people they would recover.

7 Comment on reading

People need healing when their lives have got out of order. It can be that their bodies are affected; then people may need help from a doctor or a chemist. People's feelings and emotions can become disordered too. Then they may need a doctor, but they will certainly need help, encouragement from others. People can get into trouble spiritually through sin or their own foolishness. Then they need to be helped by the grace of God. But God is also working in the other problems too: he heals in answer to prayer, but more often through the love and kindness and prayers of others. On this feast of St. Blaise, we think of the healing, the help, the new life we have received from the kindness of others.

8 Response to reading

(a) If the blessing of throats by priests or deacons is available in the area:

Announce the times and place for blessing.

(b) If the blessing of throats by a priest or deacon is NOT available in the area, then all are led to say together:

> Through the prayers of St. Blaise, bishop and martyr
> May God heal us of all ailments of the throat
> And from every other evil.
> Through Christ our Lord.
> Amen.

9 Prayers

With St. Blaise we pray:

[a]	That hospices, hospitals and surgeries may be places of love and healing.
Response:	**Send us your Holy Spirit of healing.**
[b]	That doctors and nurses, who specialise in diseases of the ear, nose and throat, may be wise and effective.
Response:	**Send us your Holy Spirit of healing.**
[c]	That the rescue services and voluntary bodies may be respected and supported by our citizens.
Response:	**Send us your Holy Spirit of healing.**
[d]	That those who have brought pain or suffering on others may seek and find forgiveness.
Response:	**Send us your Holy Spirit of healing.**
[e]	That we may bring healing love to others in their need.
Response:	**Send us your Holy Spirit of healing.**
[f]	[other prayers]
Response:	**Send us your Holy Spirit of healing.**
[g]	Our Father [perhaps sung]

10 Thought-Word-Phrase for the day

As we pass any hospital or surgery, pray "Jesus bless all in there."

11 Blessing

> May God strengthen us in faith.
> Keep us from evil,
> And help us to bring healing to others.
> Amen.

12 Concluding Song or Music

CFE		O&N
210	God gives his people strength	-
-	Our God sent his Son long ago	435

31

St Scolastica

1 Entrance music (tape or CD) Choose a suitable piece of music

2 Introduction

Scholastica was the sister of St. Benedict who was a founder of the great monastery of Monte Cassino in Italy. She, too, founded monasteries of nuns. The two used to meet once a year near Benedict's monastery. About 543 Scholastica wanted to prolong the yearly visit, but he wished to hurry back. She prayed and the weather became so bad that Benedict could not move. They spent this last night talking about spiritual things. Three days later Scholastica died. Later Benedict was buried with her, so that even death did not separate them.

St. Scholastica is patron of Benedictine nuns.

3 Focus or symbol

- – Flipchart with the name Scholastica
- – Bible or prayer book

4 Sign of the Cross

Scholastica and Benedict gave their lives totally to God in love of Christ. And so we begin "In the name of the Father and of the Son and of the Holy Spirit."

5 Hymn or song

CFE		O&N
499	My God loves me	359

 ## 6 Reading

Luke 10:38–42
(paraphrased)

One time Jesus was invited to stay with two sisters, Martha and Mary. Mary was concerned with serving Jesus; Mary instead of helping her sister, sat at the feet of Jesus listening to him. When Martha got upset, Jesus said to her, "Martha you are upset about many things; Mary has chosen just one thing, which will not be taken from her."

7 Comment on reading

There can often be misunderstandings in families, as various members see things in different ways, or want to do different things. St. Scholastica as a nun was one who often wanted to listen to God. In our lives we can be too busy, so that we do not make time for prayer and for listening. Jesus wants our hearts and our attention more than anything we might think of doing for him.

8 Response to reading

Let us think of our own family. How can I be more sensitive or caring?

9 Prayers

We trust in God's love and care and with St. Scholastica we pray.

[a] That family life may be strengthened in our land.
Response: **You are our joy and our hope.**

[b] That families that are divided may rediscover love.
Response: **You are our joy and our hope.**

[c] That family members who must live apart may be remembered with kindness.
Response: **You are our joy and our hope.**

[d] That the great monastic families of Sts. Benedict and Scholastica may continually teach the Church how to pray and to listen to the Lord.
Response: **You are our joy and our hope.**

[e] That we would learn to listen in silence to Jesus.
Response: **You are our joy and our hope.**

[f] [other prayers]
Response: **You are our joy and our hope.**

[g] Our Father [perhaps sung]

10 Thought-Word-Phrase for the day

"I turned to God who heard my prayer"

St. Scholastica

11 Blessing

Lord watch over us this day.
May we love you and others in all that we say and do.
Amen.

12 Concluding song or music

CFE		O&N
597	Peace perfect peace	-
or		
-	Sing a simple song unto the Lord	481

Our Lady of Lourdes

1 Entrance music (tape or CD) Choose a suitable piece of music

2 Introduction

In 1858 Mary appeared to a very poor girl Bernadette Soubirous near Lourdes in the south of France. She gave a message that people should do penance, pray and ask for healing. Lourdes has since become one of the great places of pilgrimage in the world.

3 Focus or symbol

- Image of the Virgin Mary and/or Rosary beads

4 Sign of the Cross

Mary showed Bernadette, and other people she appeared to elsewhere, how to make the Sign of the Cross properly, and so we begin, "In the name of the Father and of the Son and of the Holy Spirit. Amen."

5 Hymn or song

CFE		O&N
263	Holy Virgin by God's decree	218
or		
300	Immaculate Mary	-

 ## 6 Reading
John 2:1–10
(paraphrased)

There was a wedding in the town of Galilee called Cana. Jesus' mother was there. The wine gave out and Mary noticed it and brought the problem to the attention of Jesus, "They have no wine left," she said. She told the attendants to do whatever Jesus said. He then changed a huge amount of water into the finest wine.

7 Comment on reading

Years after the apparition when she was a nun in a convent, Bernadette wrote a letter describing what happened in Lourdes. "I saw a Lady wearing a white dress with a blue sash. She had a yellow rose on each foot, and her rosary was the same colour. The Lady spoke to me on several occasions and asked me to come each day for a fortnight. She asked that a chapel be built at the place. She told me to drink. Not seeing any water I turned back to go down to the River Gave to drink, but she pointed to a tiny spring that only had a little dirty water. After scratching at the spring eventually there was some water to drink. When I asked her who she was she told me she was the Immaculate Conception."

That spring became a stream in which many now bathe. Many people use Lourdes water in faith. It is a place of prayer and pilgrimage, at which many people come into healing of body, mind or spirit.

8 Response to reading

We listen to Mary's words to those at the feast, "Do whatever he tells you." What is Jesus asking us to do or to avoid today?

9 Prayers

We pray for healing and blessing for others and for ourselves.

[a]   We pray for all pilgrims who jour-ney to Lourdes in search of healing and peace.
Response: **Open our hearts to your love.**

[b]   We pray for all the sick and for those who love and care for them.
Response: **Open our hearts to your love.**

[c]   We pray for the healing of the nations.
Response: **Open our hearts to your love.**

[d]   We pray for all who take risks for peace.
Response: **Open our hearts to your love.**

[e]   We pray for ourselves that we may be peacemakers.
Response: **Open our hearts to your love.**

[f]   [other prayers]
Response: **Open our hearts to your love.**

[g]   Our Father [perhaps sung]

10 Thought-Word-Phrase for the day

Mary's words:

"Do whatever he tells you"

11 Blessing/prayer

Lord may we receive your gifts in purity of heart; may they bring us healing and peace, now and always. Amen.

From the Missal

12 Concluding song or music

CFE		O&N
-	My soul proclaims the Lord my God	368
or		
684	Magnificat, magnificat	734
or		
849	My soul glorifies the Lord	-

St Valentine

1 Entrance Music (tape or CD) Choose a suitable piece of music

2 Introduction

St. Valentine's Day is a great secular feast, with the custom, heavily promoted by commercial interests, of those in love sending cards. There were several saints by the name of Valentine, and so their relics are venerated in Churches: the forearm in Glasgow, the body in Dublin and some important relics in the Roman Church of St. Praxedes. One of the Valentines was a Roman priest martyred about 259. He was honoured with a great Church in Rome within a hundred years. The other Valentine was an Italian bishop who was martyred about the same time; hence there arose confusion between the two saints.

Valentine is the patron saint of lovers. The custom of sending cards on the feast originates in the belief found in the Middle Ages that birds paired off in the middle of February.

3 Focus or symbol

- Picture or symbol of bird
- A Valentine card

4 Sign of the Cross

Martyrs make the greatest possible sacrifice by dying for Christ who died for them on the Cross, and so we begin "In the name of the Father and of the Son and of the Holy Spirit."

5 Hymn or song

CFE		O&N
499	My God loves me	359

 6 Reading *John 15:12–14*
(paraphrased)

The night before he dies Jesus said to his apostles, "My command is this: love one another, just as I love you. The greatest love is to lay down one's life for one's friends. And you are my friends if you do what I command you."

7 Comment on reading

Christianity is a religion about love and friendship. We are to love Jesus, and be his friends. We are to love one another. But love is not a passing feeling, something I have until I go off the person. The most genuine love is lasting. But for love to last, people have to be willing to sacrifice for one another. Selfishness destroys love and friendship. Jesus who died for us is our greatest friend.

8 Response to reading

In silence ask Jesus to bless somebody that we love.

9 Prayers

With St. Valentine we turn to the God of love and pray.

[a]   We pray for engaged couples, that their love may grow and mature.

Response: **Jesus you call us your friends.**

[b]   We pray for families, that they may be prepared to make the sacrifices needed to nourish love.

Response: **Jesus you call us your friends.**

[c]   We pray for single-parent families, that they would find support in God and in others.

Response: **Jesus you call us your friends.**

[d]   We pray for those who have been disappointed in love, that their hearts may not be bitter and that they will find love again.

Response: **Jesus you call us your friends.**

[e]   We pray for ourselves that we may be generous and loyal in loving.

Response: **Jesus you call us your friends.**

[f]   [other prayers]
Response: **Jesus you call us your friends.**

[g]   Our Father [perhaps sung]

10 Thought-Word-Phrase for the day

True love is generous

11 Blessing   *2 Corinthians 13:13*

The grace of our Lord Jesus Christ, the love of God and the fellowship of the Holy Spirit be with us all.
    Amen.

12 Concluding song or music

CFE		O&N
730	This is my body	-
or		
-	The love I have for you, my Lord	536

St David

1 Entrance music (tape or CD) Choose a suitable piece of music

2 Introduction

St. David is the principal patron saint of Wales. The Welsh form of the name is Dafydd. He founded several strict monasteries, the principal one being St. David's in Pembrokeshire. Monks came from Ireland and all parts of Britain to study under him. He was bishop of Minevia and died either in 588 or in 601.

Even in Shakespeare's time there was a custom of Welsh people wearing leeks or daffodils on his feast. But the origin of this practice is not known.

3 Focus or symbol

- Daffodil or leek
- Map of Wales

4 Sign of the Cross

In the Cross is our salvation, and so we begin "In the name of the Father and of the Son and of the Holy Spirit."

5 Hymn or Song

CFE		O&N
684	Tell out my soul	514

6 Reading   *Matthew 5:14–16*

In the Sermon on the Mount Jesus taught "You are like light for the whole world. A city built on a hill cannot be hidden. No one lights a lamp and puts it under a bowl; instead he puts it on the lamp-stand, where it gives light for everyone on the house. In the same way your light must shine before people, so that they will see the good things you do and praise your Father in heaven."

7 Comment on reading

The Christian Church has no politics. Rather good Christians are to be found in all parties. The Bible tells us that we are to be good citizens in whatever country we find ourselves. We should be proud of our origins. Today we celebrate with the people of Wales their national feast. We ask God's blessing on that part of Britain and we give thanks for its culture and Christian heritage. We are reminded of the need to be light to the world.

8 Response to reading

A leek/daffodil and a paper Cross are pinned to the map of Wales.
A daffodil could be presented to any pupil or teacher with the name David, or who comes from Wales.

9 Prayers

With St. David we raise our hearts in prayer.

[a]	We ask God's blessing on the Welsh Assembly.
Response:	**May we be light to the world.**
[b]	We pray for the Welsh Royals and for all the people of Wales.
Response:	**May we be light to the world.**
[c]	We give thanks for Welsh language and culture.
Response:	**May we be light to the world.**
[d]	We ask that we may be light for those around us.
Response:	**May we be light to the world.**
[e]	We seek to be light to others through our deeds.
Response:	**May we be light to the world.**
[f]	[other prayers]
Response:	**May we be light to the world.**
[g]	Our Father [perhaps sung]

10 Thought-Word-Phrase for the day

To be a light for others

11 Blessing   *2 Corinthians 13:13*

The grace of our Lord Jesus Christ, the love of God and the fellowship of the Holy Spirit be with us all.
    Amen.

12 Concluding song or music

A Welsh hymn might be chosen.

CFE		*O&N*
532	O Great St. David	-

St Patrick

1 Entrance Music (tape or CD) Celtic music

2 Introduction

Patrick was born in Britain. He was captured by Irish pirates and made a slave in Co. Antrim where he looked after herds. He escaped back to his own people after a number of years. But he heard the voice of the Irish people calling to him in a dream to come back to them. He became a bishop and returned to Ireland where he preached the Gospel for the rest of his life. He died about 461. Places associated with him are a mountain in Ireland, "Croagh Patrick," a place of pilgrimage there called "Lough Derg," and the ancient Christian town of Glastonbury. He is patron of Ireland but is venerated in many places in the world as a great preacher.

3 Focus or symbol

- – Design of shamrock leaves.
- – Images suggesting Ireland, Britain and the preaching of the gospel, such as Bible and Catechism.

4 Sign of the Cross

Patrick preached about Jesus Christ, whose Cross we honour. So we begin "In the name of the Father and of the Son and of the Holy Spirit."

5 Hymn or song

CFE		O&N
106	Christ be beside me	79
	(Hymn of Patrick)	

 ## 6 Reading
From the Confessions of St. Patrick

"When I came to Ireland I looked after herds every day and I used to pray many times during the day. More and more my love for God and my reverence for him began to increase.

My faith and my zeal grew stronger and more intense. I was full of enthusiasm. How was it that the Irish who in their ignorance worshipped idols, but now are children of God? I daily expect to be murdered or robbed or reduced to slavery in one way or another. Not that I fear any of these things. Because of his promises I leave myself in the hands of almighty God the ruler of all. I now entrust myself to God who is most faithful and for whom I am an ambassador in my lowly situation.

What return can I make for all his goodness to me? What can I say or what can I promise to my Lord since any ability I have comes from him. To God be glory forever."

7 Comment on reading

There are many things we can learn from Patrick. Perhaps today we might think of his great love for Christ and his strong desire to preach about him. Moreover he loved the Irish who had treated him so badly. He saw Christ in everyone. He found his mission often difficult, but he trusted in God and kept going, no matter what opposition he met. The shamrock is an image of the Trinity. Patrick was above all a man of faith, devoted totally to loving and making known the Father, Son and Holy Spirit.

8 Response to reading

Make some sign of honour for the bible and the *Catechism* in which we find the faith, e.g. holding them up, lighting a candle before them.

9 Prayers

We give thanks for the gift of faith.

[a] We pray for all who work to spread the Gospel.
Response: **Christ be beside us.**

[b] We pray for continuing peace and justice in these islands, especially in the North of Ireland.
Response: **Christ be beside us.**

[c] We pray for harmony and good race relations.
Response: **Christ be beside us.**

[d] We pray for refugees and exiles.
Response: **Christ be beside us.**

[e] We pray for all unjustly imprisoned.
Response: **Christ be beside us.**

[f] [other prayers]
Response: **Christ be beside us.**

[g] Our Father [perhaps sung]

10 Thought-Word-Phrase for the day

"Christ be with me, wherever I go."

Prayer ascribed to Patrick

11 Blessing *2 Corinthians 13:13*

The grace of our Lord Jesus Christ, the love of God and the fellowship of the Holy Spirit be with us all.
    Amen.

12 Concluding song or music

CFE		O&N
234	Hail glorious St. Patrick	191
or		
106	Christ be beside me	79

41

St Joseph

1 Entrance music (tape or CD) Choose a suitable piece of music

2 Introduction

St. Joseph was a carpenter. He was husband of the Virgin Mary and he was foster-father of Jesus. Because he looked after Jesus and Mary so well he is patron of the Church. Because he was a carpenter, he is patron of all tradespeople, especially those who work with wood.

3 Focus or symbol

- – Some symbol of carpentry: hammer, nails, wood, saw.

4 Sign of the Cross

St. Joseph because holy through looking after Jesus: we become holy through our baptism, "In the name of the Father and of the Son and of the Holy Spirit."

5 Hymn or song

YOC		O&N
37	St. Joseph was a carpenter	–

6 Reading   *Matthew 1:18,20–21*

This is how the birth of Jesus Christ took place. His mother Mary was engaged to Joseph, but before they were married she found out that she was going to have a baby by the Holy Spirit. An angel of the Lord appeared to Joseph in a dream and said, "Joseph, descendant of David, do not be afraid to take Mary to be your wife. For it is by the Holy Spirit that she has conceived. She will have a son, and you will name him Jesus–because he will save his people from their sins."

7 Comment on reading

When God brought about his great plan for the salvation of all, which was sending the Son to come among us, Joseph did not know what he was to do. He was engaged to Mary, but what about this wonder-child that Mary had conceived by the Holy Spirit? Joseph was at a loss. He prayed and tried to think up plans. But the angel guided him: it was to be all so simple. He was to take Mary, adopt the child as if it were his own; he was to play out his ordinary life as a father, husband, carpenter. Later when he died, it seems that Mary and Jesus were still alive. That is why he is also called the Patron of a Happy Death, because his death was beautiful, surrounded by Mary and Jesus.

8 Response to reading

We learn from St. Joseph that God's plan for us is usually to do all the ordinary things well. We learn too that St. Joseph protects the Church just as he protected the Holy Family. We can ask him to help those who are dying.

9 Prayers

With St. Joseph we trust in God's plan for us as we pray:

[a] We are concerned for the Church that it may be protected and holy.
Response: **Jesus, Mary and Joseph hear our prayer.**

[b] We think of all the needs of families.
Response: **Jesus, Mary and Joseph hear our prayer.**

[c] We remember those who are very sick and dying, especially in our local hospital.
Response: **Jesus, Mary and Joseph hear our prayer.**

[d] We pray for all that work hard, especially those who work in buildings and make furniture.
Response: **Jesus, Mary and Joseph hear our prayer.**

[e] We are touched by the problems people have who have no work.
Response: **Jesus, Mary and Joseph hear our prayer.**

[f] We ask for a blessing on our school, on our teachers, parents and all who work here.
Response: **Jesus, Mary and Joseph hear our prayer.**

[g] [other prayers]
Response: **Jesus, Mary and Joseph hear our prayer.**

[h] Our Father [perhaps sung]

10 Thought-word-phrase for the day

To talk to Jesus, Mary and Joseph some time today about my family

11 Blessing   *2 Corinthians 13:13*

The grace of our Lord Jesus Christ, the love of God and the fellowship of the Holy Spirit be with us all.
Amen.

12 Concluding song or music

CFE		O&N
235	Hail, holy Joseph, hail!	-
or		
-	Dear St. Joseph	118

43

The Annunciation

1 Entrance music (tape or CD) Choose a suitable piece of music

2 Introduction

Today we celebrate the time when the Angel Gabriel appeared to Mary and told her that God wanted her to become the Mother of Jesus, the Messiah. Although Mary was fearful and puzzled by this, she said "yes" to God. This feast links us with the great feast of Christmas, nine months later. We recall this feast when we say the Angelus or the first of the mysteries of the Rosary.

3 Focus

- – Poster/artefact/painting of the Annunciation scene

4 Sign of the Cross

The sign of the Cross is a holy act, and so we begin "In the name of the Father and of the Son and of the Holy Spirit."

5 Hymn or song

CFE		O&N
-	When Mary listened to God's word	611
or		
236	Hail Mary full of grace	-
or		
686	The Angel Gabriel	-

6 Reading

Luke 1:26–38
(paraphrased)

God sent the Angel Gabriel to a town in Galilee named Nazareth. He had a message for a girl engaged to Joseph. Her name was Mary. The angel came and said, "Rejoice, the Lord has greatly blessed you." Mary was very disturbed by this message, and she wondered what it meant. The angel assured her. He told her not to be afraid;… God had blessed her; …the Holy Spirit will come upon her;… She will have a child named Jesus; …nothing is impossible with God. Mary then said that she was happy to be the Lord's servant.

7 Comment on reading

We are used to seeing nice pictures of Mary, perhaps at prayer and the angel. But we forget what a fright she must have got. At the Annunciation she would have been about twelve years old, and she is told that she has been chosen from all women to be the Mother of the long-awaited Messiah. The angel had to reassure her, and her love of God overcame her fear. She said a total "yes" to God. All faith in the Church is based on the example of Mary's generous "yes."

8 Response to reading

We all say "yes" in our hearts to God.

Some pupils bring flowers and lay them at the picture of Mary.

9 Prayers

We turn to our loving Father and pray with Mary.

[a] That the Church may be strengthened in faith.
Response: **Holy Mary, Mother of God, pray for us sinners, now and at the hour of our death.**

[b] That the angel's words, "nothing is impossible to God" may give courage to all who work for peace and justice.
Response: **Holy Mary, Mother of God, pray for us sinners, now and at the hour of our death.**

[c] That Christians may allow the Holy Spirit to come upon them.
Response: **Holy Mary, Mother of God, pray for us sinners, now and at the hour of our death.**

[d] That all who are fearful and all who live alone may be kept safe.
Response: **Holy Mary, Mother of God, pray for us sinners, now and at the hour of our death.**

[e] That we may say "yes" to God's plan for us.
Response: **Holy Mary, Mother of God, pray for us sinners, now and at the hour of our death.**

[f] [other prayers]
Response: **Holy Mary, Mother of God, pray for us sinners, now and at the hour of our death.**

[g] Our Father [perhaps sung]

10 Thought-word-phrase for the day

To say with Mary.
"Yes, Lord Jesus"

11 Blessing

May the Lord bless us.
May his light guide us;
May his love draw us.
Amen.

12 Concluding music or song

CFE		O&N
-	O Mary, when our God chose you	407
or		
538	O Lady full of God's own Grace	-
or		
808	Where are you bound, Mary	-

45

St Anselm

1 Entrance music (tape or CD) Choose a suitable piece of music

2 Introduction

St. Anselm was born about 1033 in the North West of Italy. After a restless youth he became a monk at Bec in Normandy (France). In 1093 he became Archbishop of Canterbury. He had on several occasions to stand up for the rights of the Church against two kings. He was an important theologian and is one of the doctors of the Church, that is, a group of thirty-three saints whose teaching occupies a special place in its tradition and life.

3 Focus or symbol

- Picture/outline drawing of a boat or ship, since Anselm was a great defender of the Church.

- *Catechism of the Catholic Church.*

4 Sign of the Cross

St. Anselm continually preached about God's love and mercy, which is shown forth in the Cross, and so we begin "In the name of the Father and of the Son and of the Holy Spirit."

5 Hymn or song

YOC		CFE
138	Father we love you… (Glorify your name)	-
or		
-	Let there be love	358
or		
-	This little light	736

6 Reading   *Matthew 5:14–16*

In the Sermon on the Mount Jesus taught "You are like light for the whole world. A city built on a hill cannot be hidden. No one lights a lamp and puts it under a bowl; instead he puts it on the lamp-stand, where it gives light for everyone on the house. In the same way your light must shine before people, so that they will see the good things you do and praise your Father in heaven."

7 Comment on reading

In his great poem in Paradise the great Italian poet Dante placed Anselm among the spirits of light. His teaching was light to the Church of his time and since. He was very much concerned to show people how reasonable and important it is to believe in God and to have faith. We too must be prepared o help people understand why we believe and have faith in God. As the centre of the Anglican Communion, the Archbishop of Canterbury is one of the great Church leaders not only in Britain, but also in the whole Christian world.

8 Response to reading

Light a candle to symbolise the light of faith.

9 Prayers

We come to our God with confi-dent prayer.

[a]   We pray for universities and places of learning.
Response: **Jesus, you are the light of the world.**

[b]   We pray for monasteries.
Response: **Jesus, you are the light of the world.**

[c]   We pray for the Archbishop of Canterbury and for Anglicans everywhere.
Response: **Jesus, you are the light of the world.**

[d]   We pray for those who find faith difficult.
Response: **Jesus, you are the light of the world.**

[e]   We pray that we may be a light for others.
Response: **Jesus, you are the light of the world.**

[f]   [other prayers]
Response: **Jesus, you are the light of the world.**

[g]   Our Father [perhaps sung]

10 Thought-Word-Phrase for the day

Make me hunger and thirst for you alone, O God

From prayer of St. Anselm

11 Blessing

May the blessings of generosity
light,
peace and
love
be in our hearts this day and always.
     Amen.

12 Concluding song or music

CFE		O&N
S11	Christ be our light *(Supplement)*	-
or		
S12	Walk in the light *(Supplement)*	305/547

St George

1 Entrance music (tape or CD) Choose a suitable piece of music

2 Introduction

St. George was a fourth century martyr much venerated in the Christian East. Pictures of St. George often show him overcoming a great dragon, a legendary animal that has always symbolised evil. George was a Christian warrior without fear. English crusaders in the Middle Ages discovered devotion to George and brought it back to England. He has been patron of England at least from the time of Edward III and the building of the Chapel of St. George at Windsor about 1348.

3 Focus or symbol

- A St. George Cross, which is a red cross against a white background.

4 Sign of the Cross

Through the Cross we can overcome evil and so we begin "In the name of the Father and of the Son and of the Holy Spirit."

5 Hymn or song

CFE		O&N
765	Walk with me O my Lord	582

6 Reading

Romans 12:9–21
(extracts)

Love must be completely sincere. Hate what is evil, hold on to what is good. Serve the Lord with a heart full of devotion. Be happy with those who are happy, weep with those who weep. Have the same concern for everybody. If someone has done you wrong, do not repay with wrong. Do everything possible to live in peace with everybody. Never take revenge. Do not let evil defeat you, instead conquer evil with good.

7 Comment on reading

The Christian life is a struggle between good and evil. It is usually more important to consider what is good and beautiful than to be focused on what is wrong. But it is also important at times to look squarely at evil—in our own lives and around us—and ask God's help to overcome it. St. George and the Dragon are a symbol of the power of good to defeat evil. But courage is involved and patience in the ongoing struggle.

8 Response to reading

Draw attention to the St. George Cross and pray silently for some person or people suffering at this time from evil.

9 Prayers

God of all nations and peoples we turn to you with our needs, confident that you will help us to overcome evil.

[a]   That all peoples may live in
           harmony and peace.
Response: **Lord bless our land.**

[b]   That leaders in our country may
           serve the good of all.
Response: **Lord bless our land**

or in England:

[b]   That the Royal Family may be
           examples for all.
Response: **Lord bless our land.**

[c]   That the Church may be bold in
           proclaiming Christ.
Response: **Lord bless our land.**

[d]   That we may recognise the evil and
           sin in our lives and try to overcome
           it.
Response: **Lord bless our land.**

[e]   That we may love our country and
           respect all its citizens.
Response: **Lord bless our land.**

[f]   [other prayers]
Response: **Lord bless our land.**

[g]   Our Father [perhaps sung]

10 Thought-Word-Phrase for the day

Deliver us from evil

11 Blessing

May God the Father protect us.
May Jesus our brother be close
   to us.
May the Holy Spirit be our Helper
   and Guide.
   Amen.

12 Concluding song or music

CFE		O&N
352	Leader now on earth no longer	296

St Mark

1 Entrance music (tape or CD) Choose a suitable piece of music

2 Introduction

St. Mark is one of the four Gospel writers or evangelists. His gospel, the shortest of the four, seems to have been based on vivid personal memories of the apostle, St. Peter. Mark was an early missioner, a companion for a while of St. Paul, identified with John Mark in the Acts of the Apostles.

St. Mark is patron of Venice and of notaries. His symbol is the lion.

3 Focus or symbol

- Bible open at the Gospel of St. Mark, perhaps on a drape with a plant.

4 Sign of the Cross

Making the sign of the Cross is a holy act, and so reverently we begin "In the name of the Father and of the Son and of the Holy Spirit."

5 Hymn or song

CFE		O&N
268	How lovely on the mountains	223/224

 ## 6 Reading

Acts 15:36-40 (paraphrased)

There was a painful disagreement among the first great missionaries of the Church. Barnabas wanted to take Mark on a missionary journey, but Paul did not think it was right, as Mark had not kept going to the end on a previous mission. After a sharp argument, Barnabas took with him the weaker Mark, whilst Paul took a sturdier figure, Silas.

7 Comment on reading

There is nothing unusual about disagreements. There are often different ways of looking at or doing things. In this reading Paul did not want the faint-hearted Mark for a difficult mission. But though there was a disagreement, they later made it up, as we read that when Paul was in prison, Mark was a companion, serving him faithfully (see Col. 4:10).

8 Response to reading

We give thanks for the gift of God's truth in the gospel by renewing our confession of faith.

Leader:	Do you believe in God, our Loving Father?
All:	We do believe.
Leader:	Do you believe in Jesus, our Way, our Truth and our Life?
All:	We do believe.
Leader:	Do you believe in the Holy Spirit, our Helper and Guide?
All:	We do believe.

9 Prayers

Confident that God always hears us, we pray.

[a] That bishops, priests, deacons, teachers and parents may be good witnesses to the Gospel.

Response: Make us witnesses of the Good News.

[b] That those who study the scriptures may serve the Church in truth.

Response: Make us witnesses of the Good News.

[c] That all who suffer because of their faith may be given strength by God.

Response: Make us witnesses of the Good News.

[d] That families may always be places of love, forgiveness and reconciliation.

Response: Make us witnesses of the Good News

[e] That we may have a deep love for holy Scripture.

Response: Make us witnesses of the Good News.

[f] [other prayers]

Response: Make us witnesses of the Good News.

[g] Our Father [perhaps sung]

10 Thought-Word-Phrase for the day

We have the Good News about Jesus Christ

Mark 1:1

11 Blessing

May Jesus bless us with forgiving hearts and with generous spirits. Amen.

12 Concluding song or music

CFE		*O&N*
202	Go tell it on the mountains	187

St Catherine of Siena

1 Entrance music (tape or CD) Choose a suitable piece of music

2 Introduction

St. Catherine was born in the Italian city of Siena in probably 1347. She was a member of a very large family of twenty children. From an early age she wanted to give her whole life to God. She cut off all her hair to discourage young men who wanted to marry her. She lived a sort of hermit life as an associate member of the Dominican Order, but even though she learned to read and write only shortly before her death, she was an advisor of popes. She travelled much in seeking to reconcile people who were at war. Her profound mystical works led to her being declared one of the thirty-three doctors of the Church who are its special teachers. She developed the idea of the bridge we must cross to God, which is an ever-deepening love.

St. Catherine is the patron saint of office workers.

3 Focus or symbol

- Bridge
- File or some other office equipment

4 Sign of the Cross

Catherine is known as the mystic of the blood of Jesus, and so we recall his Cross by beginning, "In the name of the Father and of the Son and of the Holy Spirit."

5 Hymn or song

CFE		O&N
-	Jesus, I love you	278
or		
830	You shall cross the barren desert	-
or		
662	Sons of God	-

 6 Reading   *Luke 10:38–42*
(paraphrased)

One time Jesus was invited to stay with two sisters, Martha and Mary. Mary was concerned with serving Jesus; Mary instead of helping her sister, sat at the feet of Jesus listening to him. When Martha got upset, Jesus said to her, "Martha you are upset about many things; Mary has chosen just one thing, which will not be taken from her."

7 Comment on reading

St. Catherine was a great mystic who spent much time in prayer. But she was also active in serving the poor, making peace between cities at war and looking after sinners. She had great love for the Church and its priests. It is always difficult to find time for work and time for prayer. The greatest saints, like Catherine, managed to reflect something of the prayerful, listening attitude of Mary, with active service of Jesus, which characterises Martha.

8 Response to reading

We think in silence: how much time do I spend in prayer? Is it enough?

9 Prayers

God gave St. Catherine great love. With her we pray.

[a]	For all members of the Church.
Response:	**Lord, teach us to love and to pray.**

[b]	For all who have been hurt in the Church or by the Church.
Response:	**Lord, teach us to love and to pray.**

[c]	For all office workers.
Response:	**Lord, teach us to love and to pray.**

[d]	For all with learning difficulties and for those who help them.
Response:	**Lord, teach us to love and to pray.**

[e]	For ourselves that we may be peacemakers.
Response:	**Lord, teach us to love and to pray.**

[f]	[other prayers]
Response:	**Lord, teach us to love and to pray.**

[g]	Our Father [perhaps sung]

10 Thought-Word-Phrase for the day

Being friends of Jesus

11 Blessing   *Numbers 6:24–26*

May the Lord bless and take care of you.
May the Lord be kind and gracious to you.
May the Lord look on you with favour and give you peace.
    Amen.

12 Concluding song or music

CFE		O&N
154	Eye has not seen	-
or		
-	For you are my God	252

St Joseph the Workman

1 Entrance music (tape or CD) Choose a suitable piece of music

2 Introduction

This main feast of St. Joseph, husband of the Virgin Mary and adoptive father of Jesus, occurs on 19 March. Pope Pius XII created to-day's feast in 1955 to remind the Church of the importance of work and of the dignity that all should have, no matter what their employment.

As we celebrate the feast of Joseph the Patron of Workers, we remember also those who are unemployed or retired.

3 Focus or symbol

- Picture or image of St. Joseph
- Name of some local firms

4 Sign of the Cross

Lord Jesus show us the way to the Father as we begin "In the name of the Father and of the Son and of the Holy Spirit."

5 Hymn or song

CFE		O&N
627	St. Joseph, God has chosen you	-
or		
-	Joseph was an honest man (esp. st.3)	288

6 Reading
Colossians 3:23

Whatever you do, work at it with all your heart, as though you were working for the Lord and not for others.

7 Comment on reading

Since God wants us to work according to our possibilities, our attitudes to work, to people and to the environment should be that of Christ. We must never look down on people because of what they do, or because they have no work. The Christian is one who respects people whatever their race, class, religion or position. In society we need so many people working so that we can live: we need people to grow food, drive buses, make things, work at home—thousands of jobs make life easy for all of us. Jesus regards work done for others as done for himself (see Matthew 25).

8 Response to reading

Teachers and other staff members are presented with a flower to show that we are grateful for what they do.

9 Prayers

Asking St. Joseph to pray with us we come before God with our needs.

[a]	For all whose work is difficult and dangerous.
Response:	**Bless our work.**

[b]	For skilled and unskilled workers.
Response:	**Bless our work.**

[c]	For those who give safe and healthy employment.
Response:	**Bless our work.**

[d]	For those who are retired, redundant or unemployed.
Response:	**Bless our work.**

[e]	For ourselves as we work and play.
Response:	**Bless our work.**

[f]	[other prayers]
Response:	**Bless our work.**

[g]	Our Father [perhaps sung]

10 Thought-Word-Phrase for the day

Respect for all we meet

11 Blessing

Bless us and all at work this day.
Strengthen us with your love and peace.
Help us to support and encourage one another.
Amen.

12 Concluding song or music

YOC		*O&N*
37	St. Joseph was a carpenter	-

Sts. Philip and James

1 Entrance music (tape or CD) Choose a suitable piece of music

2 Introduction

Today we celebrate the feasts of two apostles, close disciples of Jesus in his public life and witnesses to his death and resurrection. We do not have many details about either of their lives. Philip was from the town of Bethsaida. He was a disciple of John the Baptist, but later followed Jesus. In the gospels he is the apostle who usually asks what looks like a foolish question, or says something that is not correct, which allows Jesus to develop his true teaching. James was the name of two saints in the early Church. One, called James the Greater perhaps because he was older, was especially intimate with Jesus along with Peter and John. He is venerated in Compostella in Spain. The other, James the Less, honoured today with Philip, is thought to be the author of the New Testament book called The Letter of James: it is full of practical advice on how to be a genuine Christian.

3 Focus or symbol

- A bible open at the Letter of St. James
- Crucifix

4 Sign of the Cross

The apostles were martyred, taking up the Cross of Jesus, and so we begin "In the name of the Father and of the Son and of the Holy Spirit."

5 Hymn or song

CFE		O&N
175	Follow me, follow me	145

6 Reading
John 14: 6, 8–10
and James 2:14.26 (paraphrased)

Jesus said, "I am the Way, the Truth and the Life; no one comes to the Father except by me." Philip said to him, "Show us the Father; that is all we need." Jesus answered, "For a long time I have been with you all; yet you do not know me Philip? Whoever has seen me has seen the Father."

James teaches us still when he wrote, "What good is it, my brothers and sisters, if you say you have faith and do not have works. Faith without works is dead."

7 Comment on reading

Philip asks to see the Father. But he is told to look at Jesus who shows us the heart of the Father. James instructs us about good works. The Christian life is about faith, which sees, and good works, which is love.

8 Response to reading

Ask the pupils what they take from the notion that God is Father. Write a few of the ideas on flipchart/overhead. In silence pray to God in our favourite image.

9 Prayers

With the apostles, Philip and James, we turn to Jesus who is the Way, the Truth and the Life and pray.

[a] That people may open their minds and hearts to the call of Jesus.
Response: **Jesus, you are the Way to the Father.**

[b] That leaders of Church and state may see things from God's point of view.
Response: **Jesus, you are the Way to the Father.**

[c] That all who suffer for love of Jesus may be given strength.
Response: **Jesus, you are the Way to the Father.**

[d] That we may be genuine followers of Christ by believing and doing good.
Response: **Jesus, you are the Way to the Father.**

[e] That we will all spread the Good News about Jesus even by the way we live.
Response: **Jesus, you are the Way to the Father.**

[f] [other prayers]
Response: **Jesus, you are the Way to the Father.**

[g] Our Father [perhaps sung]

10 Thought-Word-Phrase for the day

Knowing Jesus and the Father

11 Blessing

Bless us this day with the love of the Father and of the Son and of the Holy Spirit.
Amen.

12 Concluding song or music

CFE		O&N
543	Centre of my life	-
or		
-	Our God sent his Son long ago	435

St Bede the Venerable

1 Entrance music (tape or CD) Choose a suitable piece of music

2 Introduction

St. Bede, called "the Venerable" even during his own lifetime, was born in 673 near the monastery of Jarrow which he later joined. Though he never seems to have travelled outside his native Northumbria, he was perhaps the most learned man of his day being a recognised expert in theology, the scriptures, botany, astronomy, mathematics, sacred history and literature. He wrote the first History of the English People, and was busy translating the Bible into Old English at the time of his death.

3 Focus or symbol

- Candle
- Map of England with Jarrow marked
- Encyclopaedia

4 Sign of the Cross

In the Cross of Christ we find the wisdom of God and so we begin "In the name of the Father and of the Son and of the Holy Spirit."

5 Hymn or song

CFE		O&N
S11	Christ be our light (Supplement)	-
or		
-	We see the Lord	599

6 Reading

Matthew 5:14–16

In the Sermon on the Mount Jesus taught "You are like light for the whole world. A city built on a hill cannot be hidden. No one lights a lamp and puts it under a bowl; instead he puts it on the lamp-stand, where it gives light for everyone on the house. In the same way your light must shine before people, so that they will see the good things you do and praise your Father in heaven."

7 Comment on reading

We will be judged by God not on what we know, but on how deeply we believe, how strongly we hope, how genuinely we love. Today we celebrate a great scholar, the only English saint to be a doctor of the Church, that is a group of thirty-three saints whose teaching is part of the Church's richest heritage. But it was not for all his learning that Bede was called "Venerable," but mainly because he was a good man.

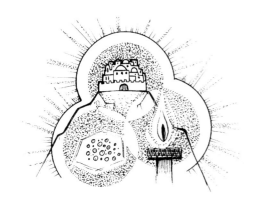

8 Response to reading

Ask ourselves: what do we value or admire most in other people? What should people value or admire in us?

9 Prayers

With St. Bede we pray for our country and for ourselves.

[a]   For scholars and institutes of learn-
             ing.
Response: **Christ, you are our light.**

[b]   For monasteries and places of
             prayer and peace.
Response: **Christ, you are our light.**

[c]   For those in prison and places of
             detention.
Response: **Christ, you are our light.**

[d]   For those trapped in anger, dark-
             ness or sin.
Response: **Christ, you are our light.**

[e]   For ourselves in our needs.
Response: **Christ, you are our light.**

[f]   [other prayers]
Response: **Christ, you are our light.**

[g]   Our Father [perhaps sung]

10 Thought-Word-Phrase for the day

We are the light of Christ

11 Blessing

Bless us today with the light of your
    Holy Spirit.
        Amen.

12 Concluding song or music

CFE		YOC
388	Shine, Jesus shine (Lord, the light of your love is shining)	81

St Augustine of Canterbury

1 Entrance music (tape or CD) Choose a suitable piece of music

2 Introduction

There are two famous saints with the name Augustine. One is Augustine of Hippo in North Africa whose feast is 28 August. Today we celebrate the feast of St. Augustine of Canterbury. He was a monk in Rome when Pope Gregory I in 596 sent him as a missionary to England. Accompanied by thirty monks, he arrived in Kent, where he was in time well received by the Southern Kings of England, beginning with Ethelbert who was, however, at first cautious. He established a major church in Canterbury, which became the principal diocese in England. [Today the principal Anglican diocese remains Canterbury; the main Catholic diocese is Westminster.] Augustine was a careful missionary: he did not destroy pagan temples that people were used to worshipping in, instead he blessed them and used them for Christian worship. A saying ascribed to him reflects this policy: "Anyone, who wants to climb to a great height must go by steps, not leaps."

3 Focus or symbol

- – Bible
- – Overhead/flipchart with caption "Apostle of England."
- – Picture of Canterbury

4 Sign of the Cross

Augustine is often pictured arriving on the shore following a Cross carried by monks. So we begin "In the name of the Father and of the Son and of the Holy Spirit."

5 Hymn or song

CFE		O&N
633	Seek ye first the kingdom of God	473

6 Reading *Matthew 9:37*

Jesus said to his disciples, "The harvest is large, but there are few workers to gather it in. Pray to the owner of the harvest that he would send out workers to gather in his harvest."

7 Comment on reading

As we travel around we can find many old churches and ruins of monasteries. These are reminders of those who brought the faith, lived it with courage, even to dying for it. Today we are grateful to missionaries who bring the faith to those who do not know Christ. We give thanks for our own faith.

8 Response to reading

The need to have the patience to take small steps to achieve anything worthwhile. What small steps can I take today?

9 Prayers

We turn to God and pray.

[a]   For bishops, priests and religious, that they may be faithful.
Response: **Seek the Lord always.**

[b]   For missionaries, clerical, religious and lay, that they may have health and live in safety.
Response: **Seek the Lord always.**

[c]   For an increase of labourers to gather the Lord's harvest.
Response: **Seek the Lord always.**

[d]   For the Anglican Communion and the Diocese of Canterbury.
Response: **Seek the Lord always.**

[e]   For our parents and for all who love us.
Response: **Seek the Lord always.**

[f]   [other prayers]
Response: **Seek the Lord always.**

[g]   Our Father [perhaps sung]

10 Thought-Word-Phrase for the day

The great gift of faith

11 Blessing

Lord of the harvest bless us this day, increase our faith, hope and love.
    Amen.

12 Concluding song or music

YOC		CFE
23	In the earth a small seed is hidden	306

The Visitation

1 Entrance music (tape or CD) Choose a suitable piece of music

2 Introduction

This feast, from the word "visit," celebrates the journey of Mary to her cousin Elizabeth and their meeting. The Franciscans began to celebrate it in 1263, and it spread in the Church during the following century.

3 Focus

- Poster/artefact/painting of the Visitation scene
- Text of the Magnificat (or at least opening few lines) on overhead (Luke 1:46–55)

4 Sign of the Cross

The Cross proclaims the greatness of God's love and mercy for each one of us and so we begin "In the name of the Father and of the Son and of the Holy Spirit."

5 Hymn or song

CFE		O&N
849	My soul glorifies the Lord	-
or		
YOC		
40	An angel came from heaven	-
or		
-	My soul proclaims the Lord my God	368
or		
-	Magnificat settings	364
-		365
-		368

6 Reading
Luke 1:39–56
(extracts, paraphrased)

After the Annunciation Mary went to the hill country of Judea to visit her cousin Elizabeth whom she had learned from the angel was also to become a mother. Mary's greeting was grace-filled. Immediately Elizabeth and her unborn son, John the Baptist, were blessed and filled with the Holy Spirit. Elizabeth praises Mary, saying "Blessed are you among women and blessed is the fruit of your womb." She then says that Mary is blessed because she believed the angel. Mary celebrates God's great work in her—My soul praises the Lord, my soul is glad because of God my Saviour; she celebrates God's love for his people—"He shows mercy to those who honour him;" she recalls God's love for the poor—"He brought down the mighty from their thrones and lifted up the lowly, filling the hungry with good things;" she proclaims that God's favour to her will be forever remembered–"From now on all people will call me happy because of the great things God has done for me."

7 Comment on reading

The effect of Mary's greeting, probably Shalom ("Peace") was dramatic: Elizabeth and her child are blessed. This is because Mary brought Jesus to the house of Elizabeth. Mary brings Jesus into all our lives. If we are close to Jesus, we will bring blessings too. Mary brought practical help to Elizabeth: companionship, help with housework, joy in the Lord.

8 Response to reading

We receive many visits from Jesus in the Eucharist, the scripture, prayer, through one another.

Raise up the bible whilst all sing in response:
"Glory and praise to you O Lord,
You are the Word of God."

9 Prayers

We come before our loving God who blessed Mary, and blesses us as we pray.

[a]	For people who risk their lives on missions of charity; we remember in particular the Red Cross, Médicin sans Frontières, and relief organisations (*name local ones*)
Response:	**The Lord has done great things for us.**
[b]	For all unborn children; we remember their mothers and families.
Response:	**The Lord has done great things for us.**
[c]	For those who bless others by a smile, a word or kind deed; we remember those who have been good to us.
Response:	**The Lord has done great things for us.**
[d]	For the gift of hospitality; we remember times when we were made welcome.
Response:	**The Lord has done great things for us.**
[e]	For a generous spirit for ourselves; we remember our homes and our school.
Response:	**The Lord has done great things for us.**
[f]	[other prayers]
Response:	**The Lord has done great things for us.**
[g]	Our Father [perhaps sung]

10 Thought-word-phrase for the day

Think of ways to bless or bring joy to others

11 Blessing   *Jude v2*

May mercy, peace and love be yours today, in full measure.
Amen.

12 Concluding music or song

CFE		O&N
849	My soul proclaims the Lord my God	368
or		
-	Magnificat settings 364,365,368	

The Sacred Heart

1 Entrance music (tape or CD) Choose a suitable piece of music

2 Introduction

Today we are invited to ponder what we so often take for granted, that God loves us. We focus on the Heart of Jesus. Who loved us even to the point of dying for us. In most cultures the heart is the symbol of love; it is what is deep inside us. We speak of a person having a kind heart, or a hard heart.

When the Church was gripped with fear of God's anger, a French sister, St. Margaret Mary Alacoque, was given visions of the Sacred Heart in 1673 which assured us that God loves us and that we are to serve without excessive fear. At the same time, we must be careful about sin and pray for those who sin.

3 Focus or symbol

- Picture, poster, artefact of the Sacred Heart.
- Overhead with prayer, "Sacred Heart of Jesus, we place our trust in you."

4 Sign of the Cross

The Heart of Jesus was pierced with a sword as he died, and so we begin, "In the name of the Father and of the Son and of the Holy Spirit."

5 Hymn or song

CFE		O&N
499	My God loves me	359

6 Reading   *1 John 4:7–9, 11–12*

Dear friends, let us love one another because love comes from God. Whoever loves is a child of God and knows God. Whoever does not love, does not know God, for God is love. God showed his love for us by sending his only Son into the world, so that we might have life through him. No one has ever seen God, but if we love one another God lives in us and his love is made perfect in us.

7 Comment on reading

Love is a word that is much used and often badly used. Love is not a feeling, but it is rather the fact that we do good things for other people, such as forgiving them, helping them, showing them kindness. If we love others, then we can get a better idea of how God loves us. We think of this great love.

8 Response to reading

Symbols of God's love are carried in and held high:

> The Bible which is God's love-letter to his people.
> The Cross by which we see God's love for us.
> The chalice which reminds us of Jesus' love for us in the Mass and Holy Communion.

As a response to such great love we pray the overhead prayer: "Sacred Heart of Jesus, we place our trust in you.

9 Prayers

We turn to the God of love and pray.

[a] That we would open our hearts to your gifts.
Response: **Heart of Jesus we trust in you.**

[b] That we would open our hearts to welcome you in others.
Response: **Heart of Jesus we trust in you.**

[c] That we would open our hearts to comfort others.
Response: **Heart of Jesus we trust in you.**

[d] That we would open our hearts in forgiving others.
Response: **Heart of Jesus we trust in you.**

[e] That we would open our hearts to the needs of the poor.
Response: **Heart of Jesus we trust in you.**

[f] [other prayers]
Response: **Heart of Jesus we trust in you.**

[g] Our Father [perhaps sung]

10 Thought-word-phrase for the day

Receive God's love today

11 Blessing

May the love of Jesus surround us.
May the love of Jesus forgive us.
May the love of Jesus help us to love one another.
   Amen.

12 Concluding music or song

CFE		O&N
570	Oh the love of my Lord	430
or		
167	Father, we love you	-
or		
-	The love I have for you my Lord	536
or		
553	O Sacred Heart	428

St Charles Lwanga and his companions

1 Entrance music (tape or CD) Choose a suitable piece of music

2 Introduction

St Charles and his twenty-one companions are the first martyrs in Africa south of the Sahara. They were from Uganda, which had Christian missionaries from about 1880. A great persecution broke out under King Mwanga in 1885 and Charles and other court officials with a lot of teenage Christians were put to death for the faith. There were Anglican martyrs put to death at the same time.

3 Focus or symbol

- Cross
- Map of Africa indicating Uganda
- Artefact of African culture

4 Sign of the Cross

The martyrs died for Christ who had died for them and so we begin "In the name of the Father and of the Son and of the Holy Spirit."

5 Hymn or song

CFE		O&N
147	Do not be afraid for I have redeemed you	122

6 Reading   *Matthew 5: 10–12*

Happy are those who are persecuted because they do what God requires; the kingdom of heaven belongs to them! Happy are you when people insult you and persecute you and tell all kinds of evil lies against you because you are my followers. Be happy and glad, for a great reward is kept for you in heaven.

7 Comment on reading

The Ugandan Martyrs were put to death partly because they were Christian, but more particularly because they stood up to the king who had done many evil things, and had previously killed an Anglican missionary, James Hannington. It is very easy to allow ourselves to drift into doing wrong things just because our companions or even close friends do something evil. It requires great courage to stand back and refuse to follow bad example.

8 Response to reading

Pray silently for the courage to stand firm for Christ. Teacher may hold up a bible for all to see.

9 Prayers

We pray for missionaries and those who suffer for their faith.

[a] For people who even today suffer for following Christ's teaching.
Response: **Make us strong to stand firm.**

[b] For the people of Africa at this time, who suffer much from poverty and wars.
Response: **Make us strong to stand firm.**

[c] For those treated as slaves and forced to do cruel work.
Response: **Make us strong to stand firm.**

[d] For young people today that they may be strong in saying no to drugs and violence.
Response: **Make us strong to stand firm.**

[e] For ourselves that we may be strong in standing for Christ in work and play.
Response: **Make us strong to stand firm.**

[f] [other prayers]
Response: **Make us strong to stand firm.**

[g] Our Father [perhaps sung]

10 Thought-Word-Phrase for the day

"Stand firm in the faith"

1 Corinthians 16:13

11 Blessing   *Numbers 6:24–26*

May the Lord bless and take care of you.
May the Lord be kind and gracious to you.
May the Lord look on you with favour and give you peace.
   Amen.

12 Concluding song or music

CFE		O&N
739	Though the mountains may fall	569
or		
816	Yahweh I know you are near	-

St Columba or Colmcille

1 Entrance music (tape or CD) Choose a suitable piece of music

2 Introduction

St Columba, also called Colmcille ("the Dove of the Church") was born in Donegal, Northwest Ireland about 521. He was from a royal family in Ireland, but became a monk. He founded many monasteries, eventually ending up on the island of Iona, still today a place of pilgrimage and prayer. He was rather too hard on himself and others as a young monk, but he mellowed with years so that people found him very approachable. He was known for his love of all living creatures and is remembered as a poet, healer, and as the Founder of the Celtic Church.

3 Focus or symbol

- Dove on overhead/flipchart, with the name Columba/Colmcille
- Map with pointer to Iona [and Northwest Donegal in Ireland]

4 Sign of the Cross

St. Columba wrote a prayer, "The path I walk, Christ walks it," and so we begin "In the name of the Father and of the Son and of the Holy Spirit."

5 Hymn or song

CFE		O&N
729	This day God gives me [from words of St. Patrick]	555

6 Reading

from the Life of St. Columba by Adomnan, monk at Iona.

When he was forty-three he sailed away from Ireland to Britain wishing to be a pilgrim for Christ. During the thirty-four years he spent as a soldier of Christ on the island, he could not let any hour pass that was not given to prayer, reading, writing or some other good work. He seems to be able to do the work of several men at the one time, yet through all he was loving to everybody, his face was always cheerful and he was happy in his heart with the joy of the Holy Spirit.

7 Comment on reading

Holy people are not distant, hard or unattractive. We tend nowadays to speak about "good people" rather than "holy people," but the reality is the same. Columba was dedicated wholly to God, but people found him attractive. A little poem from the Irish language is often said to reflect the spirit of Columba. It is about a cat called Pangur Bán (pronounced bawn, which means, "white").

> I and Pangur Bán my cat,
> 'Tis a like task we are at:
> Hunting mice is his delight,
> Hunting words I sit all night.

8 Response to reading

With St. Columba we learn the importance of balance in our lives. He divided his time between prayer, reading and good works. We need time for prayer, time to help others, time for study, time for play. Columba loved animals and simple things. It is easy to miss out on simple pleasures like seeing a spider walk, a bird eating, a cat relaxing, a playful dog, a baby smiling, the leaves on a branch, clouds, a flower…

9 Prayers

We turn to the God of gentleness and with St. Columba pray.

| [a] | For the people of Ireland and Scotland at this time. |
| Response: | **Open our hearts to the wonder of your love.** |

| [b] | For missionaries everywhere. |
| Response: | **Open our hearts to the wonder of your love.** |

| [c] | For all who work to protect the environment. |
| Response: | **Open our hearts to the wonder of your love.** |

| [d] | For all pilgrims, especially people who find life difficult at this time. |
| Response: | **Open our hearts to the wonder of your love.** |

| [e] | For ourselves that we may be grateful for our baptism and for all the gifts we have received through others. |
| Response: | **Open our hearts to the wonder of your love.** |

| [f] | [other prayers] |
| Response: | **Open our hearts to the wonder of your love.** |

| [g] | Our Father [perhaps sung] |

10 Thought-Word-Phrase for the day

Respect for all living creatures

11 Blessing   *Prayer of St. Columba*

Be a bright flame before me,
A guiding star above me,
A smooth path below me,
A kindly shepherd behind me.
   Amen

12 Concluding song or music

CFE		O&N
106	Christ be beside me	79

St Barnabas

1 Entrance music (tape or CD) Choose a suitable piece of music Allowed

2 Introduction

St. Barnabas was one of the most attractive saints in the New Testament. He came to the Jewish religion in Cyprus and joined the early Christian communities at Jerusalem and later in Antioch. He was a missioner along with St. Paul in the cities of the Eastern Mediterranean. His name was changed by the apostles from the much respected Jewish name of Joseph to Barnabas, which was taken to mean "Son of Encouragement." Indeed, wherever we come across the his tracks in the New Testament, Barnabas is usually encouraging others, even the great Paul.

St. Barnabas is the patron saint of Cyprus.

3 Focus or symbol

- The name Barnabas on overhead/flipchart
- Large envelope with words "well done" on outside

4 Sign of the Cross

The early Church gathered around the Good News that "Jesus is Lord," and so we begin in the power of his Cross, "In the name of the Father and of the Son and of the Holy Spirit."

5 Hymn or song

YOC		CFE
18	Give thanks	189

 6 Reading   *Acts 11:19–30*
(paraphrased)

When there was a persecution in Jerusalem not many years after the Resurrection and Pentecost, Christians moved up the coast to Antioch in modern Turkey. There a flourishing community developed.
The Church leaders in Jerusalem sent Barnabas to see how things were getting on. He saw the work of God and he encouraged them to continue. He saw that they could do with a strong teacher, so he went to look for Saul, now called Paul, who had himself been a persecutor. He brought Paul to the Church in Antioch. The leaders trusted Barnabas and Paul and sent them on an important task to Jerusalem.

7 Comment on reading

In various places in the New Testament we come across Barnabas. He is usually encouraging and supporting people. Even the great Paul, the brilliant writer of New Testament letters and fearless missioner around the Mediterranean, needed Barnabas to speak for him to make him acceptable to the leaders in Antioch. Barnabas was a person who could see good everywhere. In Antioch he had the eyes to see the great things that God was doing.

8 Response to reading

Am I an encourager? Do I always think of saying thanks, at home, at school, on the bus, in shops? Everybody likes and needs a word of encouragement. I might sometimes say to a teacher, "thank you, I enjoyed that lesson today." I should keep an eye open to praise people for things they do. There is a saying that we get a donkey to move easier with a carrot, which it likes, than with a stick. Carrots in our daily lives can be kindly words.

9 Prayers

With St. Barnabas we try to look with fresh eyes on the world around us.

[a]	We thank you for so much good that is in our world.
Response:	**We give you thanks, O Lord.**
[b]	We thank you for people who lift us up through music, art, and literature.
Response:	**We give you thanks, O Lord.**
[c]	We thank you for those who entertain us, footballers, and stars of the film and pop world, writers, and TV presenters.
Response:	**We give you thanks, O Lord.**
[d]	We thank you for those who cheer us up and make us laugh.
Response:	**We give you thanks, O Lord.**
[e]	We thank you for those who make us feel better.
Response:	**We give you thanks, O Lord.**
[f]	[other prayers]
Response:	**We give you thanks, O Lord.**
[g]	Our Father [perhaps sung]

10 Thought-Word-Phrase for the day

Say "well done" to somebody today

11 Blessing   *2 Corinthians 13:13*

The grace of our Lord Jesus Christ, the love of God and the fellowship of the Holy Spirit be with us all.
      Amen.

12 Concluding song or music

CFE		*O&N*
685	Thank you for giving me the morning	-
or		
-	Thank you	515

St Anthony of Padua

1 Entrance Music (tape or CD) Choose a suitable piece of music

2 Introduction

One of the best-loved saints in the Western Church is St. Anthony who was born in Lisbon, Portugal, but ministered most of his life in Northern Italy, dying in the city of Padua in 1231. He was a Franciscan friar who became an outstanding preacher. He was noted for his outstanding love for those who were poor or destitute. In some countries today, the poor box in the church is named "St. Anthony's Bread." He was noted for his love of animals, and there is a very popular devotion to him as the patron of lost articles. For his time he had a remarkable knowledge of the bible. His sermons which were very rich in Christian doctrine led to him be listed among the Doctors of the Church.

3 Focus or symbol

- Bible

4 Sign of the Cross

Anthony was a great preacher of God's love shown to us in the death of Jesus and so we begin "In the name of the Father and of the Son and of the Holy Spirit."

5 Hymn or song

CFE		O&N
799	Whatever you do	606

6 Reading

James 2:1–13
(paraphrased)

You must not let social differences affect the way you treat people. Thus you should not treat a rich person with greater respect, or ignore a poor person. Those who are poor may be better people and have more faith. Indeed sometimes the rich may cause you more trouble than poor people. You must love your neighbour as yourself. If you are not merciful to others, God will not be merciful to you. If you are kindly to others, you will not have anything to worry about before God.

7 Comment on reading

One of the strongest commandments taught in the Bible is love for those who are poor. It is not that they are necessarily better, but they are more helpless and do not have as good a chance of doing well as those who are more fortunate. St. Anthony was known for his great love for those in need. Indeed in some places there is a popular belief that if we lose something and promise a small offering for the poor, St. Anthony will help us to find the missing item more quickly! This is not Church teaching, but it does tell us something about the heart of Anthony, and is a humourous reminder of a great truth, which is that we should always be generous to those less well off than ourselves.

8 Response to reading

Place a box in the assembly place where each pupil and teacher can place one coin tomorrow for some local need, if possible in such a way that they are not seen doing so.

9 Prayers

We pray for the needs of the Church and the world.

[a]   We pray for all groups who look after poor people.

Response: **Teach us Lord to be generous.**

[b]   We pray for those in government that they may have a care for those in need.

Response: **Teach us Lord to be generous.**

[c]   We pray for all who are in serious need.

Response: **Teach us Lord to be generous.**

[d]   We pray for those who have no homes.

Response: **Teach us Lord to be generous.**

[e]   We pray that we would respect all people, those who are poor and those who are rich.

Response: **Teach us Lord to be generous.**

[f]   [other prayers]
Response: **Teach us Lord to be generous.**

[g]   Our Father [perhaps sung]

10 Thought-Word-Phrase for the day

Give thanks for what I have

11 Blessing   *Numbers 6:24–26*

May the Lord bless and take care of you.
May the Lord be kind and gracious to you.
May the Lord look on you with favour and give you peace.
      Amen.

12 Concluding song or music

CFE		*O&N*
227	God's Spirit is in my heart	183

St Alban

1 Entrance music (tape or CD) Choose a suitable piece of music

2 Introduction

St. Alban is venerated as the first British martyr. Little is known about the circumstances of his life. He is thought to have died about 209 or up to a century later. Devotion to him had a long tradition in England with churches and monasteries dedicated to him. St. Alban's in Essex, and Ely are particularly associated with him. In Wales he is remembered on this day with two other British martyrs Sts. Julius and Aaron who died in Caerleon about 304.

3 Focus or symbol

- Overhead with the name Alban – in Wales also Julius and Aaron
- Map with St. Alban's highlighted – in Wales also Caerleon
- Crucifix

4 Sign of the Cross

Jesus said, "I have kept those you have given me true to your name," and so we begin "In the name of the Father and of the Son and of the Holy Spirit."

5 Hymn or song

CFE		O&N
147	Do not be afraid	122

 6 Reading *1 Peter 3:14–17 (paraphrased)*

Even if you have to suffer for doing what is right, it is very good. You should not go about afraid of people, but you should look to Christ and have respect for him as Lord. You should be ready to tell people how much Jesus means to you and how you really believe in heaven. But the ways we share our faith should be gentle and respectful. It is better to suffer hardship for doing good, that to suffer for doing wrong.

7 Comment on reading

Sometimes we will find life unfair. We do our best and then we get blamed for it. Things do go wrong. But we should not go about fearfully. We have to learn to take the good and the bad in life. In particular the martyrs remind us that we must be prepared to put up with trouble when we are doing good. Sometimes the best response to trouble is humour.

8 Response to reading

Invite pupils to name ways in which they can show that they follow Christ at home, in school in the neighbourhood. Some of these could be written on a chart. Invite pupils to pray for God's help in doing something today that is a little hard, but which pleases Jesus.

9 Prayers

We pray to God asking the help of the martyr's prayers too.

[a]	That all who suffer for Christ's sake may be blessed.
Response:	**If the Lord is on our side, who can be against us.**
[b]	That Christians may have the courage of the martyrs when trials come.
Response:	**If the Lord is on our side, who can be against us.**
[c]	That those who are unjustly in jail may be comforted.
Response:	**If the Lord is on our side, who can be against us.**
[d]	That our system of justice may have genuine values of compassion and mercy.
Response:	**If the Lord is on our side, who can be against us.**
[e]	That we would always love the Church even when its teaching seems difficult.
Response:	**If the Lord is on our side, who can be against us.**
[f]	[other prayers]
Response:	**If the Lord is on our side, who can be against us.**
[g]	Our Father [perhaps sung]

10 Thought-Word-Phrase for the day

Humour when things go wrong

11 Blessing

May the Lord strengthen us this day with the courage of the martyrs.
May we be generous even when things are hard.
Amen.

12 Concluding song or music

CFE		O&N
295	If God is for us	231

Sts John Fisher and Thomas More

1 Entrance music (tape or CD) Choose a suitable piece of music

2 Introduction

The Church celebrates two great Englishmen who were put to death for the Catholic faith in 1535. It was at the time of the reformation when Henry VIII wanted the Church to change its law for him. Both of them were learned men who wanted to be good citizens and good Catholics. But when Henry made too many demands on their conscience both preferred death to infidelity to the Catholic faith. John Fisher, a Yorkshireman, was bishop of Rochester. Thomas was a lawyer, who led a most Christian family life. During his life he held the highest political and legal offices in the land. He died saying, "I die the King's good servant, but God's first."

3 Focus or symbol

- – Bible
- – Map of England
- – Picture of Houses of Parliament or Tower of London

4 Sign of the Cross

Thomas More and John Fisher stood firm for Christ, even when threatened with death, and so we begin "In the name of the Father and of the Son and of the Holy Spirit."

5 Hymn or song

CFE		O&N
376	Look around you	316

6 Reading

From a letter of St. Thomas More from prison to his daughter

I trust in God's merciful goodness that as his grace has made me strong up to now and made me content in my heart to lose goods, land and life too, rather than swear against my conscience. Nothing can come but that which God wills. I am convinced that whatever comes, even though it seems evil, will be in fact the best.

7 Comment on reading

These two great saints stood firm for the Christian faith. They trusted that they were better citizens to oppose the plans of Henry VIII than to give in to his will. Because they were so important, the Lord Chancellor and Bishop of Rochester, Henry was not prepared to let their disapproval of his act go unpunished. We all meet situations when we should stand for Christ rather than give way. There will be times when others will encourage us to join them in doing something wrong. It is then that we need to ask God's help.

8 Response to reading

We say together the prayer of St. Thomas More:

> Give me, Good Lord, a full faith,
> a firm hope,
> a fervent love and
> a longing for you.

9 Prayers

With faith and trust we pray

[a]   That bishops may teach the truth of Christ.
Response: **We are your witnesses, O Christ.**

[b]   That judges and lawyers may be wise and just.
Response: **We are your witnesses, O Christ.**

[c]   That all in public office will consider things from Christ's point of view.
Response: **We are your witnesses, O Christ.**

[d]   That those who suffer for the truth may be strong in faith.
Response: **We are your witnesses, O Christ.**

[e]   That we would never put money or our comfort before Jesus and his Church.
Response: **We are your witnesses, O Christ.**

[f]   [other prayers]
Response: **We are your witnesses, O Christ.**

[g]   Our Father [perhaps sung]

10 Thought-Word-Phrase for the day

To be a good Christian and a good citizen

11 Blessing   *Numbers 6:24–26*

> May the Lord bless and take care of you;
> May the Lord be kind and gracious to you;
> May the Lord look on you with favour and give you peace.
> Amen.

12 Concluding song or music

CFE		O&N
568	O Lord, my God	-
or		
-	My Lord, my Master	361

St Peter and St Paul

1 Entrance music (tape or CD) Choose a suitable piece of music

2 Introduction

Sts. Peter and Paul are linked together in the Roman Church. Peter, once called Simon, was appointed leader of the apostles by Jesus. But he was often rash and he denied Jesus at the Passion. But after the resurrection Jesus asked him three times for his love. Paul, known as Saul, was a Jew who at first persecuted the Church, but was converted when travelling to Damascus. The feast of his Conversion is celebrated on 25 January. Both are seen as great protectors of the faith of the Church, and we can say that the Church is founded on them. In very solemn actions the Pope claims to speak in the name, that is, with the authority, of Peter and Paul.

St. Paul is honoured as patron of public relations. St.Peter is patron of fishermen.

3 Focus or symbol

- Boat
- Keys
- Bible open at letters of St. Paul
- Picture of Pope, St. Peter's in Rome

4 Sign of the Cross

Paul was put to death by being beheaded. Peter was crucified. We begin "In the name of the Father and of the Son and of the Holy Spirit."

5 Hymn or song

CFE		O&N
688	The Church's one foundation	518

 ## 6 Reading *Matthew 16:13–19*
(paraphrased)

When Jesus asked whom his disciples thought he was, Peter answered that Jesus was the Messiah, the Son of God. Jesus then said to Peter, "Good for you, Simon, Son of John! For this truth did not come to you from any human being, but it was given to you directly by my Father in heaven. So I tell you Peter: You are a rock and on this rock foundation I will build my church, and not even death will be able to overcome it. I will give you the keys of the kingdom of heaven." He then said that what Peter bound on earth would be bound in heaven, and what Peter loosed on earth would be loosed in heaven.

7 Comment on reading

Though Christ is said in the New Testament to be the cornerstone of the Church and of our faith (Eph 2:20; 1 Peter 2:6), the rest of the Church is made from frail humans. But Jesus promised to be with his Church until the end of the world (Matthew 28:20), and he continues to strengthen weak people to be leaders of the Church. Some popes were very sinful, but the majority of them were good, even outstanding men.

8 Response to reading

Draw attention to overhead/flipchart carrying the words, "Do you love me Peter?" How do we answer this question?

9 Prayers

With the apostles Peter and Paul we pray.

[a]   We pray for the Church that it may be true to the faith of the apostles.
Response: **We believe in one, holy, catholic and apostolic Church.**

[b]   We pray for the Pope that he may be strong in faith and leadership.
Response: **We believe in one, holy, catholic and apostolic Church.**

[c]   We pray for Christians, who are separated, that all may be one.
Response: **We believe in one, holy, catholic and apostolic Church.**

[d]   We pray for those who have been hurt by the Church in any way.
Response: **We believe in one, holy, catholic and apostolic Church.**

[e]   We pray for fishermen and for all that provide us with food.
Response: **We believe in one, holy, catholic and apostolic Church.**

[f]   [other prayers]
Response: **We believe in one, holy, catholic and apostolic Church.**

[g]   Our Father [perhaps sung)

10 Thought-Word-Phrase for the day

Jesus, Son of the Living God

11 Blessing
adapted from The Roman Missal

May the Lord who built the Church on Peter's faith bless us with a faith that never stumbles.
May the keys of Peter and the words of Paul lead us to our home in heaven.
    Amen.

12 Concluding song or music

YOC		O&N
38	Simon Peter, Simon Peter	-

St Thomas Apostle

1 Entrance music (tape or CD) Choose a suitable piece of music

2 Introduction

There are few details known about the life of the apostle St. Thomas who was called "the Twin" by the early Church, and "Doubting Thomas" in popular Christianity. He seems to have kept up the morale of the apostles in the final journey to Jerusalem where Jesus was to die. But when the other apostles said that they had seen Jesus risen, Thomas doubted. For him seeing and touching were necessary before he would believe. But when Jesus did appear to him he expressed his deep faith in the prayer "My Lord and my God."

St. Thomas is the patron of architects and of the Church in India, where he is said to have ministered.

3 Focus or symbol

- Poster of the Resurrection
- Bible open at John 20
- Map with pointer on Southwest India, home of the Thomas Christians

4 Sign of the Cross

Faith in Jesus and the marks of the Cross on his body led Thomas to faith and so we begin "In the name of the Father and of the Son and of the Holy Spirit."

5 Hymn or song

CFE		O&N
568	O Lord my God	-
or		
-	My Lord, my Master	361

6 Reading
John 20:24–29

One of the Twelve disciples, Thomas (called the Twin) was not with them when Jesus came. So the other disciples told him, "We have seen the Lord!" Thomas said to them, "Unless I see the scars of the nails in his hands and put my finger on those scars and put my hand in his side, I will not believe." A week later the disciples were together again indoors, and Thomas was with them. The doors were locked, but Jesus came and stood among them and said, "Peace be with you." Then he said to Thomas, "Put your finger here, and look at my hands; stretch out your hand and put it in my side. Stop your doubting, and believe!" Thomas answered him, "My Lord and my God!" Jesus said to him, "Do you believe because you see me? How happy are those who believe without seeing me!"

7 Comment on reading

There is a difference between seeing and believing. We believe many things that we do not see or experience. We believe that Britain is an island; we believe the label on a can of peas; we believe in other people's love for us. We believe also in God and in what we are taught through the Church. True belief is not just saying "yes" to a statement, but a yes with our lives, just as Mary did when the angel appeared to her. She said a "yes" to what God said, to what God promised, to what God willed. Mary did not see, but she was the first of those who are blessed for believing without seeing.

8 Response to reading

A Bible or a poster of the Resurrection is held up. All say, "My Lord and my God."

9 Prayers

We pray with faith and trust in the Risen Lord.

[a]	That all who receive the gift of faith may give thanks.
Response:	**Risen Christ we believe in you.**
[b]	That Christians may understand more fully the gift of holy Baptism.
Response:	**Risen Christ we believe in you.**
[c]	That those who have lapsed from the faith may find the help they need.
Response:	**Risen Christ we believe in you.**
[d]	That Indian Christians may be blessed and kept safe from persecution.
Response:	**Risen Christ we believe in you.**
[e]	That we would keep safe our own faith in Christ.
Response:	**Risen Christ we believe in you.**
[f]	[other prayers]
Response:	**Risen Christ we believe in you.**
[g]	Our Father [perhaps sung]

10 Thought-Word-Phrase for the day

Doubt no longer but believe

11 Blessing

Bless us this day with great faith in you,
Always knowing that you are our Lord and our God.
Amen.

12 Concluding song or music

CFE		*O&N*
246	He is Lord	-
or		
-	Jesus you are Lord. Risen Christ we believe in you	286

St Benedict

1 Entrance music (tape or CD) Choose a suitable piece of music

2 Introduction

St. Benedict was born in Umbria, Italy about 480. He studied in Rome but shocked by low moral standards there, he abandoned any worldly career and became a hermit. People soon gathered around him and he founded the great monastery at Monte Cassino south of Rome. He wrote a *Rule* for his monks, a way of life still followed by thousands of Benedictine and Cistercian monks to this day. In February we celebrate the feast of his sister, St. Scholastica. Pope Paul VI declared him to be Patron of Europe in 1965.

3 Focus or symbol

- Map with pointer to Italy
- Picture of a Benedictine monastery or of Benedictine monk, e.g. the late Cardinal Hume, Archbishop of Westminster (d. 1999)

4 Sign of the Cross

Benedict loved God above all else, and so we begin "In the name of the Father and of the Son and of the Holy Spirit."

5 Hymn or song

CFE		O&N
194	Glorious God, King of Creation	163

6 Reading
from the Rule of St. Benedict

When you begin something good, you should ask the Lord with ceaseless prayer to bring it to a completion. We should ensure that God who counts us as his children would never be saddened by your evil deeds. What could be dearer to us than the Lord's invitation? See how the Lord in his love shows us the way to live. We must not prefer anything to Christ so that he can lead us to be one with him in eternal life.

7 Comment on reading

We all have many choices in life: to play one game rather than another, perhaps to take one road rather than another. But at other times there is right and wrong, and we must be careful to avoid what is sinful and anything that may be harmful to ourselves or others. Whatever we do, we should think that God looks down upon us with love, and that we should not do anything that offends him.

8 Response to reading

Consider the prayer of St. Benedict on overhead or poster. In silence select some line that strikes you.

> Give me O gracious and holy Father
> A heart to meditate on you
> Ears to hear you,
> Eyes to see you,
> A tongue to speak about you,
> Speech that is pleasing to you.
> Patience to wait for you,
> And perseverance to look for you.
> Give me O God a perfect end.

9 Prayers

We ask for God's protection and love as we pray.

[a]	For the Benedictine Order at this time
Response:	**Kind God, bless us.**
[b]	For Europe that it may keep its Christian heritage.
Response:	**Kind God, bless us.**
[c]	For all Christians who try to live God's way.
Response:	**Kind God, bless us.**
[d]	For all who guide others on their spiritual journey.
Response:	**Kind God, bless us.**
[e]	For ourselves that we stay always close to Jesus.
Response:	**Kind God, bless us.**
[f]	[other prayers]
Response:	**Kind God, bless us.**
[g]	Our Father [perhaps sung]

10 Thought-Word-Phrase for the day

The beauty of God's love

11 Blessing

Bless us this day as we try to walk in your way.
May we long for the beauty of your peace.
> Amen.

12 Concluding song or music

YOC		CFE
159	We are the Church	-
-	For the beauty of the earth	177

Our Lady of Mount Carmel

1 Entrance music (tape or CD) Choose a suitable piece of music

2 Introduction

Mount Carmel is a mountain range in the Holy Land about 25 km. long. Hermits later known as the Brothers of Our Lady of Mount Carmel settled there near the Fountain of the Prophet Elijah. They had a little chapel dedicated to Our Lady. This feast has been celebrated in the whole Church since 1726.

3 Focus

- – Mountain scene or picture of Carmelite house, e.g. Aylesford, England.
- – Overhead with "Our Lady of Mount Carmel, pray for us."
- – Brown Scapular

4 Sign of the Cross

The Cross is at the heart of our faith in Jesus and so we begin "In the name of the Father and of the Son and of the Holy Spirit."

5 Hymn or Song

CFE		O&N
652	Sing of Mary	-
-	O Mary gentle one	406

 6 Reading *Song of Songs 7:5 (paraphrased)*

Your head is held high like Mount Carmel.
Your braided hair shines like the finest satin;
Its beauty could hold a king captive.
How lovely you are, how beautiful.

7 Comment on reading

For the Jews Mount Carmel was a sign of strength and beauty. Today we think of Mary's beauty. The Carmelite Order, called after her, saw in Mary a patron–that is one whom they served and who looked after them–as well as a sister and a mother who was loving and caring. The Brown Scapular, which is two pieces of brown cloth or a medal, has for centuries been a way of expressing both Mary's care for us, and our dedication and love for her.

8 Response to reading

Look at the image of Mary. What would you like to say to her?

9 Prayers

With the support of Mary's prayers we turn to our loving God and pray:

[a]   That the Church will treasure your word and become holy.

Response: **Our Lady of Mount Carmel, pray for us.**

[b]   That all who believe in you and trust in your promises may be blessed.

Response: **Our Lady of Mount Carmel, pray for us.**

[c]   That the Carmelite Order of Brothers and Sisters may continue to teach the Church the ways of prayer.

Response: **Our Lady of Mount Carmel, pray for us.**

[d]   That all Christians may be united in heart and mind.

Response: **Our Lady of Mount Carmel, pray for us.**

[e]   That in our lives the beauty and goodness of Mary may be found.

Response: **Our Lady of Mount Carmel, pray for us.**

[f]   [other prayers]

Response: **Our Lady of Mount Carmel, pray for us.**

[g]   Our Father [perhaps sung]

10 Thought-word-phrase for the day

Mary is our Mother and Sister

11 Blessing

Bless us as we journey through this day.
May we, like Mary, treasure your words in our hearts.
    Amen.

12 Concluding music or song

CFE		O&N
51	As we come before you now	-
-	Mary most holy	347

85

Our Lady's Birthday

1 Entrance music (tape or CD) Choose a suitable piece of music

2 Introduction

Birthdays are celebrations of our uniqueness, gifts and talents. They are celebrations of who we are. We may resemble someone, but no two people in all creation are exactly the same. Today we celebrate and give thanks for Mary, our Mother. She was born to be the mother of Jesus; this was her special call and gift. Her birthday has been celebrated on this day since the 6th century.

3 Focus or symbol

– Statue, poster, icon of Mary

4 Sign of the Cross

Mary loved Jesus and kept close to him even as he was dying on the Cross. We draw close to him as we begin "In the name of the Father and of the Son and of the Holy Spirit."

5 Hymn or song

CFE		O&N
538	O Lady, full of God's own grace	-
-	O Mary, when our God chose you	407

6 Reading   *Romans 8:28–30*

We know that in all things God works for good with those who love him, those whom he has called according to his purpose. Those whom God had already chosen, he also set apart to become like his Son, so that the Son might be the first among many.

7 Comment on reading

We don't know the exact date on which Mary was born. But just as in civil society a monarch's birthday is celebrated on some day chosen for convenience, the Church picked September 8 which was near the Eastern New Year which began on the first of that month. That is a reminder to us that God's great plan to save us begins to take practical shape in the birth of the child who would be the Mother of his Son.

Today is a day when we can talk to Mary, tell her how much we owe her, and how much we would like to love her Son. That is the best birthday present we could give her.

8 Response to reading

Class representatives bring forward symbols such as card, flowers, bible and leave at the statue or image of Mary.

9 Prayers

Mary placed her trust in God even when she did not understand. We marvel at the wonder and beauty of God's love for us and pray with trust.

[a]	That all the followers of Jesus may receive the Word and live by it.
Response	**Ave, ave, ave Maria.** [perhaps sung]
[b]	That the Churches may be united through the prayers of Mary and of those who love her.
Response	**Ave, ave, ave Maria.** [perhaps sung]
[c]	That all women may be treated with respect.
Response	**Ave, ave, ave Maria.** [perhaps sung]
[d]	That we would use our gifts and talents for others.
Response	**Ave, ave, ave Maria.** [perhaps sung]
[e]	That we would learn to be brothers and sisters to one another.
[f]	[other prayers]
Response	**Ave, ave, ave Maria.** [perhaps sung]
[g]	Our Father [perhaps sung]

10 Thought-word-phrase for the day

Hail Mary full of grace,
the Lord is with you

11 Blessing

May the God of mercy bless us.
May the God of peace comfort us.
May the God of love warm our hearts.
    Amen.

12 Concluding music or song

CFE		O&N
236	Hail Mary, full of grace	-
-	O Mary, gentle one	406

Triumph of the Cross

1 Entrance music (tape or CD) Choose a suitable piece of music

2 Introduction

In the Holy Land there was a celebration from about the 5th century of the wood of the cross on which Jesus died. The feast came to Europe before 700. What we think of today is not about beams of wood, no matter how holy, but about Jesus who showed his supreme love for us by dying on the Cross.

3 Focus or symbol

- Crucifix
- Overhead with the Eucharistic Acclamation:

  "Lord by your Cross and resurrection you have set us free; you are the Saviour of the world."

4 Sign of the Cross

In Baptism we were signed with the Cross and so belong to Christ forever, and so we begin "In the name of the Father and of the Son and of the Holy Spirit."

5 Hymn or song

CFE		O&N
363	Lift high the Cross	-
-	His name is higher	211

6 Reading
John 3:14–16

Jesus said to Nicodemus, "As Moses lifted up the bronze snake on a pole in the desert (*see Numbers 21:4–9*), in the same way the Son of man must be lifted up, so that everyone who believes in him may have eternal life. For God loved the world so much that he gave his only Son, so that everyone who believes in him may not die but have eternal life."

7 Comment on reading

The text "God so loved the world that he gave his only Son" is one of the best known texts in scripture, and is a favourite on what are called "wayside pulpits", that is advertisement boards or notices outside churches which carry texts from scripture or some Christian thought. This great text tells us that at the heart of Christianity is love. God's love for us comes before all else. In fact we can say that the Christian life is nothing more than our response to God's love, a response that he makes possible by grace.

8 Response to reading

Crucifix is held up and assembly sings:

CFE		O&N
246	He is Lord	206

9 Prayers

Lord by your Cross you have set us free, so hear we ask you these prayers.

[a]   For individuals and peoples unjustly treated.
Response: **You are the Saviour of the world.**

[b]   For all who have died through violence or been hurt by racial hatred.
Response: **You are the Saviour of the world.**

[c]   For those are hungry and homeless.
Response: **You are the Saviour of the world.**

[d]   For people who have not known God's love in their lives.
Response: **You are the Saviour of the world.**

[e]   For our own following of Christ.
Response: **You are the Saviour of the world.**

[f]   [other prayers]
Response: **You are the Saviour of the world.**

[g]   Our Father [perhaps sung]

10 Thought-Word-Phrase for the day

God's love for us on Calvary

11 Blessing   *Numbers 6:24–26*

May the Lord bless and take care of you.
May the Lord be kind and gracious to you.
May the Lord look on you with favour and give you peace.
     Amen.

12 Concluding song or music

CFE		O&N
268	How lovely on the mountains	223

Our Lady of Sorrows

1 Entrance music (tape or CD) Choose a suitable piece of music

2 Introduction

We all will experience sorrow and suffering at different times in our lives. Some people have to endure almost unbearable grief: illness, death of loved ones, unemployment, difficult neighbours, bullying, war, being refugees, etc.

Today we remember how Mary was close to Jesus in times of great pain and distress for both of them. Traditionally we recall seven incidents:
The Presentation in the Temple when Simeon foretold suffering for her and her Son.
The Flight into Egypt to escape from Herod.
Jesus being lost for three days.
Mary seeing Jesus carrying the Cross.
Jesus' death on the Cross.
Jesus is taken down from the Cross.
Jesus is buried.

3 Focus or symbol

- Crucifix
- Poster/artefact/painting of the Pietà (Mary holding the dead Jesus in her arms)

4 Sign of the Cross

The Cross is a stark reminder that Jesus died that we might live. With gratitude, wonder and praise we begin "In the name of the Father and of the Son and of the Holy Spirit."

5 Hymn or song

CFE		O&N
279	I met you at the Cross	-
-	Hallelujah, my Father	199

 6 Reading *Luke 2: 33–35 (paraphrased)*

At the Presentation in the Temple Mary and Joseph were amazed at the things the old prophet Simeon said about Jesus. He blessed them and said to Mary, his mother. "This child will bring about the destruction and the salvation of many in Israel. People will be against him. Sorrow like a sharp sword will break your own heart."

7 Comment on reading

We can make Mary so beautiful and remote that we can forget that she had terrible sorrows in her life. Mary wept, but Mary was also strong. Mary had to surrender her Son on Calvary. When Jesus said about the beloved disciple, "Behold your Son," Mary received us as children instead of him. The saints never cease to marvel and say, "what an exchange?" Again, Jesus never told us that we would not meet sorrow, he did, however, promise to give us strength.

8 Response to reading

We pray in silence for those we know are in trouble at this time. As a pupil or teacher holds up the crucifix all say together the response familiar to us from the Mass: "Lord by your Cross and Resurrection you have set us free; you are the Saviour of the world."

9 Prayers

God of love, you are with us always, especially in moments of sorrow. Draw near to us now as we pray.

[a]	For all who are ill in mind or body.
Response:	**Our Lady of Sorrows pray for us.**
[b]	For all who have had to leave their homes, families or countries.
Response:	**Our Lady of Sorrows pray for us.**
[c]	For the distressed peoples of *(specify)*.
Response:	**Our Lady of Sorrows pray for us.**
[d]	For all who have to suffer for their faith and for justice.
Response:	**Our Lady of Sorrows pray for us.**
[e]	For those who find school difficult at this time.
Response:	**Our Lady of Sorrows pray for us.**
[f]	[other prayers]
Response:	**Our Lady of Sorrows pray for us.**
[g]	Our Father [perhaps sung]

10 Thought-word-phrase for the day

Mary knows the sorrows of our hearts

11 Blessing   *Numbers 6:24–26*

May the Lord bless and take care of you.
May the Lord be kind and gracious to you.
May the Lord look on you with favour and give you peace.
    Amen.

12 Concluding music or song

CFE		*O&N*
538	O Lady, full of God's own grace	399

Our Lady of Mercy, Our Lady of Ransom

1 Entrance music (tape or CD) Choose a suitable piece of music

2 Introduction

This feast is special to England. Pope Leo XIII encouraged devotion to Our Lady of Ransom in all the country's dioceses. The meaning of the feast was given as encouraging people to return to Christ. It is also the feast of the Sisters of Mercy, a worldwide institute founded on this day in Dublin by Catherine McAuley.

3 Focus or symbol

- Poster or overhead with the words: "Mercy is…"

4 Sign of the Cross

The Cross reminds us of the greatness of God's mercy, and so we begin "In the name of the Father and of the Son and of the Holy Spirit."

5 Hymn or song

CFE		O&N
369	Like a shepherd he leads his flock	727

6 Reading   (texts on mercy)

"Remembering his mercy"
(Mary's Magnificat – Luke 1:50)

"God be merciful to me a sinner"
(Tax-collector's prayer – Luke 18:13)

"Blessed are the merciful for they shall see God"
(The Beatitudes – Matthew 5:7)

"Be merciful, just as your Father is merciful"
(Sermon on the Plain – Luke 6:36).

"You must have mercy, just as you received mercy"
(Parable of Unjust Steward – Matthew 18:33).

7 Comment on reading

Mercy is at the heart of Christianity. God has shown us mercy in Christ Jesus, but he expects us to show mercy to others. Traditionally in the Church there were seven corporal and seven spiritual works of mercy (see *Catechism of the Catholic Church* art 2447–2448).

The corporal works of mercy showed how Christians were to be kind in deeds: feed the hungry; give drink to the thirsty; clothe the naked; shelter the homeless; care for the sick; visit those imprisoned; bury the dead.

The spiritual works of mercy were mostly about what we say and about our attitudes: warning those who are doing wrong; instructing the ignorant; counselling the doubtful; comforting the sorrowful; bearing wrong patiently; forgiving injuries; praying for the living and the dead.

8 Response to reading

Ask pupils "What do you think mercy is?" Write some answers down on focus poster which has the words "Mercy is..."

9 Prayers

We turn to God the source of all mercy and pray:

[a] For priests and those who receive the sacrament of reconciliation.
Response: **God is rich in mercy.**

[b] For voluntary bodies concerned with the works mercy.
Response: **God is rich in mercy.**

[c] For those who are angry, violent, depressed or otherwise need mercy.
Response: **God is rich in mercy.**

[d] For the Sisters of Mercy on their feast.
Response: **God is rich in mercy.**

[e] For an increase of Christian faith in our country.
Response: **God is rich in mercy.**

[f] [other prayers]
Response: **God is rich in mercy.**

[g] Our Father [perhaps sung]

10 Thought-word-phrase for the day

To do an act of mercy today

11 Blessing   *Jude v.2*

May mercy, peace and love be yours today, in full measure.
    Amen.

12 Concluding music or song

CFE		O&N
194	Glorious God, King of creation	163
or		
219	God of mercy and compassion	180
or		
	Taizé chant on Beatitudes	

St Vincent de Paul

1 Entrance music (tape or CD) Choose a suitable piece of music

2 Introduction

St. Vincent de Paul was born in the South of France in 1582. His parents were poor. He became a priest and gradually became aware of the profound needs of the poor in France and he dedicated his life to working for their needs. He founded an institute of priests, the Congregation of the Missions (Vincentians) and of sisters, Sisters of Charity. He set up seminaries, orphanages and hospitals. He died at the age of eighty.

He is patron of charitable organisations, e.g. The Society of St. Vincent de Paul.

3 Focus or symbol

- Names of charitable groups in the area, e.g. SVP (The Society of St. Vincent de Paul)
- Map of France or art work related to France

4 Sign of the Cross

St. Vincent de Paul used to say "God loves the poor and the lovers of the poor" and so we begin "In the name of the Father and of the Son and of the Holy Spirit."

5 Hymn or song

CFE		O&N
799	Whatsoever you do	606

6 Reading
From the writings of St. Vincent de Paul

We should not judge poor people by their clothes or by their outward appearance, or by their other capacity, as they often lack education or social graces. We should be of the same mind, and imitate what Christ did, caring for the poor, consoling them, helping them and guiding them. Christ himself chose to be born in poverty and he chose poor men to be his disciples. He himself became a servant of the poor.

7 Comment on reading

There are many ways of helping people who are poor. Mother Teresa of Calcutta is a modern example of such service. People who pay taxes are helping the poor, as the government is then able to make money and other help available in social services. But it is good for us to do individual, private things for those in need. We can at times, give money, we can pray, and we can always be polite to people no matter what their appearance may be, or even if their requests cannot be answered by us at a particular time.

8 Response to reading

Place a box in the assembly place where each pupil and teacher can place one coin tomorrow for the local St. Vincent de Paul Conference or some other charitable body in the area; if possible we should avoid being seen dropping in our coin.

9 Prayers

We call on God, Lover of the Poor and with St. Vincent de Paul pray:

[a]   For the work of St. Vincent de Paul Society throughout the world.

Response: **Jesus, you had nowhere to lay your head.**

[b]   For the Vincentian Fathers and Sisters of Charity.

Response: **Jesus, you had nowhere to lay your head.**

[c]   For all who are spiritually or economically poor.

Response: **Jesus, you had nowhere to lay your head.**

[d]   For an awareness of the needs of the poor on the part of politicians and all citizens.

Response: **Jesus, you had nowhere to lay your head.**

[e]   For the gift of generosity in our lives.

Response: **Jesus, you had nowhere to lay your head.**

[f]   [other prayers]

Response: **Jesus, you had nowhere to lay your head.**

[g]   Our Father [perhaps sung)

10 Thought-Word-Phrase for the day

"Blessed are the poor in spirit"

Matthew 5:3

11 Blessing   *Numbers 6:24–26*

May the Lord bless and take care of you.
May the Lord be kind and gracious to you.
May the Lord look on you with favour and give you peace.
    Amen.

12 Concluding song or music

CFE		O&N
290	I will never forget you	265

Sts Michael, Gabriel, and Raphael – Archangels

1 Entrance music (tape or CD) Choose a suitable piece of music

2 Introduction

In the scriptures we learn that there are angels beyond number serving God. We are given the names of three of them, and we celebrate their feast today.

Michael (meaning, "Who is like God?") is honoured as captain of all the angels, and Protector of Christian soldiers. He is patron of radiologists, the sick and paratroopers.

Gabriel (meaning "Strength of God") brought the message of salvation to Mary at the Annunciation. He is patron of communications, TV and radio workers.

Raphael (meaning "Healing of God") was the guide of the holy man Tobias in the Old Testament who became blind and later recovered his sight through the archangel. He is patron of nurses, doctors and of blind people.

3 Focus or symbol

- – Annunciation scene, e.g. poster, painting or overhead.
- – One symbol or overhead sketch for each of the groups who have archangels as patrons, i.e. radiologists / paratroopers, communications media, care of the sick / blind.

4 Sign of the Cross

Angels and archangels praise Jesus in heaven. We are united with them as we begin "In the name of the Father and of the Son and of the Holy Spirit."

5 Hymn or song

CFE		O&N
602	Praise my soul the King of Heaven	449

6 Reading   *Genesis 28:12-13*

Jacob dreamed that he saw a stairway reaching from earth to heaven, with angels going up and coming down on it. And there was the Lord standing beside him.

7 Comment on reading

from *Catechism of the Catholic Church* # 334-336

The whole life of the Church benefits from the mysterious and powerful help of the angels. In her liturgy, the Church joins with the angels to adore the thrice-holy God. From infancy to death human life is surrounded by their watchful care and intercession. Already here on earth the Christian life shares by faith in the blessed company of angels and of human beings united in God.

8 Response to reading

Sing the "Holy holy holy" heard by the prophet Isaiah and used in Mass to remind us that we are joined with the angels.

CFE		O&N
258–259	Holy, holy, holy	663–669

ST MICHAEL
WHO IS LIKE GOD?

ST GABRIEL
GOD'S FORTITUDE

ST RAPHAEL
GOD'S HEALING

9 Prayers

We turn to God Lord of angels and saints as we pray.

[a] You made angels to be your servants; help us to proclaim your word.

Response: **To you be highest glory and praise for ever.**

[b] Your praise is sung by the angels; may all people on earth praise you.

Response: **To you be highest glory and praise for ever.**

[c] You give your angels to guard and protect; be with those who travel today.

Response: **To you be highest glory and praise for ever.**

[d] Your angels sang of peace at Bethlehem; may the nations know peace.

Response: **To you be highest glory and praise for ever.**

[e] Your angels always do your will; may we be faithful to our Baptism.

Response: **To you be highest glory and praise for ever.**

[f] [other prayers]

Response: **To you be highest glory and praise for ever.**

[g] Our Father [perhaps sung]

10 Thought-Word-Phrase for the day

*The angels hymn,
"Holy, holy, holy."*

11 Blessing

King of angels bless and protect us. Draw us in love and praise of you this day.
Amen.

12 Concluding song or music

CFE		O&N
196	Glory and praise to our God	-
-	We see the Lord	599

St Thérèse of Lisieux

1 Entrance music (tape or CD) Choose a suitable piece of music

2 Introduction

Thérèse of Lisieux is one of the best-loved saints in the Church. She was only fifteen when she became a Carmelite nun at Lisieux in the north of France; she died nine years later in 1897 when she was only twenty-four. The name she had in the convent was Thérèse of the Child Jesus. She is often called "The Little Flower" a name she gave to herself, when she was writing the story of her life, the book that told the world about the graces the Lord had given her, a best-seller translated into nearly fifty languages, called *The Story of a Soul.*

3 Focus or symbol

- Image of Thérèse and/or some roses.

4 Sign of the Cross

Paintings of Thérèse often show her holding a Cross; there is also a lovely photograph of her standing beside a big cross in the grounds of the convent. We begin then, "In the name of the Father and of the Son and of the Holy Spirit."

5 Hymn or song

CFE		O&N
499	My God loves me	359

6 Reading
Matthew 18:1–3

The disciples came to Jesus, asking, "who is the greatest in the kingdom of heaven?" So Jesus called a child, made him stand in front of them, and said, "I assure you that unless you change and become like children, you will never enter the kingdom of heaven."

7 Comment on reading

Jesus is telling his disciples, who were grown-ups, that they must be like children. Jesus knew that not all children are nice, that many children are naughty, and can be mean and selfish, even violent. So what is it that Jesus wants people to copy in children? We find the answer in Thérèse. She taught the Church about what she called "her little way." This was a very important doctrine, which said that what God wants from most of us are not big things, but that we do small things well. In this way, everyone is a child. None of us can do big things for God, but all of us can surely do small things. Thérèse was so good at doing little things that she became a saint. She is very holy and God listens to her prayers, sending what she called, "a shower of roses" to the world. She knew about God so well that she is a big teacher of the whole Church, called "a doctor of the Church" (from the word *doctus/docta*, which means a learned man or woman).

8 Response to reading

Pupils from each class come with a rose and leave it at the picture of Thérèse.

9 Prayers

We pray for the Church, which Thérèse loved so much.

[a] Thérèse showed the Church how to love.

Response: **Help us to trust and love like Thérèse.**

[b] Thérèse prayed and suffered for missions and missionaries.

Response: **Help us to trust and love like Thérèse.**

[c] Thérèse taught us to serve and love God in little things.

Response: **Help us to trust and love like Thérèse.**

[d] Thérèse kept going even in difficulties and bad health.

Response: **Help us to trust and love like Thérèse.**

[e] Thérèse left an example to all laity, priests and sisters.

Response: **Help us to trust and love like Thérèse.**

[f] [other prayers]

Response: **Help us to trust and love like Thérèse.**

[g] Our Father [perhaps sung]

10 Thought-Word-Phrase for the day

Let us do little things well today

11 Blessing

The grace of our Lord Jesus Christ, the love of God and the fellowship of the Holy Spirit be with you all.
 Amen.

12 Concluding song or music

CFE		O&N
358	Let there be love shared among us	726
or		
399	Love is his word	338
or		
306	In the earth the small seed is hidden	-

Guardian Angels

1 Entrance music (tape or CD) Choose a suitable piece of music

2 Introduction

Belief in Guardian Angels is very ancient in the Church, and was strong in Saxon England. Each of us has an angel to protect and to guide us. Moslems believe that each person has two. The feast of the Guardian Angels has been celebrated in the Church for the last five hundred years.

3 Focus or symbol

- Picture of angel/prayer to Guardian Angel on overhead.

4 Sign of the Cross

Our angel's greatest joy is when we follow Jesus, and so we begin "In the name of the Father and of the Son and of the Holy Spirit."

5 Hymn or song

CFE		O&N
48	Angels we have heard on high (1st verse only)	40

6 Reading   *Matthew 18:1–2,10*

The disciples came to Jesus asking, "who is the greatest in the kingdom of heaven?" Jesus called a child, made him stand in front of them, and said, "I assure you that unless you become like children you will never enter the kingdom of heaven. See that you don't despise any of these little ones. Their angels in heaven are always in the presence of my Father in heaven."

7 Comment on reading

A beautiful teaching of the Catholic faith is that we are not alone in our struggles, in our joys and sorrows. Those in heaven are with us, praying for us: Mary, the saints and the angels. Each one of us has been given an angel to guide, protect and stay with us. Whenever we are lonely or distressed, our angel is there. And we can always talk to our angel about our situation. (see *Catechism of the Catholic Church* arts 334-336)

8 Response to reading

Let us pause for a moment so that each of us can thank our Guardian Angel for looking after us.

9 Prayers

The scripture says: "God will give orders to his angels about you; they will hold you up" and so we pray:

[a]   That we would stay free from sin and do good things today.

Response: **Angels help us to adore him.**

[b]   That those who are lonely may be comforted.

Response: **Angels help us to adore him.**

[c]   That all who travel may reach their destination safely.

Response: **Angels help us to adore him.**

[d]   That we would show reverence and respect for each other, especially in the playground.

Response: **Angels help us to adore him.**

[e]   That those in the rescue services might themselves be safe, especially fire brigades, ambulance workers, sea and air rescue service people.

Response: **Angels help us to adore him.**

[f]   [other prayers]
Response: **Angels help us to adore him.**

[g]   Our Father [perhaps sung]

10 Thought-Word-Phrase for the day

The wonder of my having a Guardian Angel

11 Blessing

O Angel of God my Guardian dear,
To whom God's love commits me here.
Ever this day be at my side,
To light to guard, to rule and guide.
     Amen.

12 Concluding song or music

CFE		O&N
45	Angel voices ever singing	-
or		
832	You who dwell in the shelter of the Lord	783
or		
-	verse 4	449

St Francis of Assisi

1 Entrance Music (tape or CD) Choose a suitable piece of music

2 Introduction

Francis is a very popular name. There are several saints called Francis, but today's is one of the most popular in the Church. He was born in Assisi in 1181. His father was a rich businessman, but Francis did not desire to be wealthy. Instead he wanted to teach people about Jesus Christ and to look after poor people and sick people. He founded a great religious Order, called the Franciscans. Francis was very fond of animals; he was a great lover of nature, but he was above all a peacemaker.

3 Focus

- – Picture of Francis/picture of nature: scene, animal or birds.

4 Sign of the Cross

Francis loved to preach about Jesus and about the way he saved us by the Cross, and so we begin, "In the name of the Father, and of the Son and of the Holy Spirit."

5 Hymn or song

CFE		O&N
191	Give me peace, O Lord, I pray	160

6 Reading   *Matthew 11:25–26*

Jesus said, "Father, Lord of heaven and earth! I thank you because you have shown to the unlearned what you have hidden from the wise and the learned. Yes Father, this is how you wanted it to happen.

7 Comment on reading

Though he had many gifts and drew many people to journey with him and to serve the poor, Francis remained always very simple in heart. He loved the simple things of life. All loved him: people, animals, birds. He saw God in all creation; he was at one with the whole of creation.

8 Response to reading

We all quietly look out the window. If we see the sky, or a cloud, a tree, a bird, or a flower, they can speak to us about God, just as they all spoke to Francis.

9 Prayers

We give thanks for all God's gifts and we pray for peace.

[a] We give thanks for the beauty of creation: animals, birds, nature, scenery, the land and sea…
Response: **Lord, help us to be loving like Francis.**

[b] We pray for reverence of ourselves and of all others.
Response: **Lord, help us to be loving like Francis.**

[c] We pray for peace throughout the world.
Response: **Lord, help us to be loving like Francis.**

[d] We pray for our planet and for the environment.
Response: **Lord, help us to be loving like Francis.**

[e] We pray for all who take risks for peace.
Response: **Lord, help us to be loving like Francis.**

[f] [other prayers]
Response: **Lord, help us to be loving like Francis.**

[g] Our Father [perhaps sung]

10 Thought-word-phrase for the day

St. Francis' prayer for peace.
It could be written into their notebooks by the children or written up on blackboards and copied, and learned at least in part by older children.

Make me a channel of your peace.
Where there is hatred, let me bring your love.
Where there is injury, let me bring pardon.
Where there is despair, let me bring hope.
Where there is darkness, let me bring light.
Where there is sadness, let me bring joy.
Oh, Master, grant that I may never seek so
*   much to be consoled as to console,*
To be understood as to understand.
To be loved as to love with all my heart.

11 Blessing   *2 Corinthians 13:13*

The grace of our Lord Jesus Christ, the love of God and the fellowship of the Holy Spirit be with us all.
Amen.

12 Concluding song

CFE		O&N
478	Make me a channel of your peace	342
or		
385	Lord, make me an instrument of thy peace	328

Our Lady of the Rosary

1 Entrance music (tape or CD) Choose a suitable piece of music

2 Introduction

Pope Pius V introduced this feast in 1573 in thanksgiving for the victory of Lepanto, which saved Christianity from being overrun by Moslems from the East. The Rosary is a devotion based on the simple prayers: *Our Father*, *Hail Mary*, *Glory be to the Father*. In reciting these prayers we think of fifteen events in the life of Jesus and we can try to see them through the eyes of Mary. They are joyful, sorrowful and glorious events or mysteries. The Dominican Order has been most associated in the Church with preaching about and promoting the Rosary.

3 Focus

- Poster/artefact/painting of Mary with Rosary in her hand
- Rosary beads

4 Sign of the Cross

Praying the Rosary with Mary brings us into the heart of the Christian mystery, and so we begin "In the name of the Father and of the Son and of the Holy Spirit."

5 Hymn or song

CFE		O&N
236	Hail Mary, full of grace	192/700
or		
YOC		
45	Hail Mary, full of grace	

6 Reading
Luke 2:19.51

After Bethlehem Mary remembered all these things and thought deeply about them… As Jesus grew up, Mary treasured all these things in her heart.

7 Comment on reading

Mary is our model of faith. She said a complete "yes" to what God said, to what God promised, to what God wanted. But she had to pray and ponder so that she would make her heart reflect God's ways. We too need to ponder and pray if we are to be followers of Jesus.

8 Response to reading

Five roses or flowers are brought to the image of Mary as the names of the Joyful Mysteries are read aloud: Annunciation, Visitation, Birth of Jesus, Presentation of Jesus, Finding in the temple.

A Crucifix is brought forward as the Sorrowful Mysteries are named: the Agony of Jesus, the Scourging, the Crowning with Thorns, the Carrying of the Cross, the Crucifixion.

A bible and/or a chalice are brought forward as the Glorious Mysteries are named: Resurrection, Ascension, Coming of the Holy Spirit, Assumption, Coronation of Mary.

9 Prayers

You invite us, O God, to say "yes" to your plan as Mary did.

[a]   That the Church may ponder deeply the mysteries of Christ.
Response: **Pray for us now and at the hour of our death. Amen.**

[b]   That the simplicity of Bethlehem may teach us not to be grabbing or greedy.
Response: **Pray for us now and at the hour of our death. Amen.**

[c]   That the Lord's Passion may give courage to those who suffer.
Response: **Pray for us now and at the hour of our death. Amen.**

[d]   That the Risen Lord will draw us all in hope.
Response: **Pray for us now and at the hour of our death. Amen.**

[e]   That with Mary we may learn to ponder the things of God in our hearts.
Response: **Pray for us now and at the hour of our death. Amen.**

[f]   [other prayers]
Response: **Pray for us now and at the hour of our death. Amen.**

[g]   Our Father [perhaps sung]

10 Thought-word-phrase for the day

Mary's big "Yes" to God

11 Blessing   *2 Corinthians 13:13*

The grace of our Lord Jesus Christ, the love of God and the fellowship of the Holy Spirit be with us all.
Amen.

12 Concluding music or song

CFE		O&N
293	I'll sing a hymn to Mary	-
-	O Mary gentle one	406

St Luke

1 Entrance music (tape or CD) Choose a suitable piece of music

2 Introduction

Luke who was the author of the Third Gospel was a physician and a companion of St. Paul on his missionary journeys. His Gospel recalls lovingly the sayings of Jesus about poor people, women and about those who were at the margins. He was also remembered as an artist in the early Church.

St. Luke is the patron of doctors and of artists.

3 Focus or symbol

- Bible opened at the Gospel of Luke
- Paintbrushes and some symbol of medicine: chart, tablets etc

4 Sign of the Cross

St. Luke shows us Jesus as very human and caring. He shows us Jesus as bravely facing the his death on the Cross as he journeyed to Jerusalem, and so we begin "In the name of the Father and of the Son and of the Holy Spirit."

5 Hymn or song

CFE		O&N
582	Open your ears O Christian people	422

 6 Reading *Luke 1:1–4 (paraphrased)*

Luke dedicated his Gospel to a Roman Theophilus. He told him that many people had done their best to write a report of what Jesus did and said. This gospel was carefully handed down. Now Luke studied all these matters again and wrote an orderly account for Theophilus, so that he would know the full truth about what he had been taught.

7 Comment on reading

Each of the gospels has a particular interest or way of looking at the story of Jesus. The story of our salvation is a mystery that can never be fully described. The account of St. Luke is in many ways the most human portrait of Jesus and the Lord's concern for the poor. At various times we will look at Jesus differently, now thinking about his love, his mercy, his power, his promises, his teaching, his compassion, his suffering, his glory... The four Gospels in their own way can always feed our minds and hearts.

8 Response to reading

Some pupils tell their favourite passages of the life of Jesus.

9 Prayers

We turn to the compassionate God and pray.

[a]   That all who read the Gospel may know God's deep love for us.
Response: **Jesus is Lord.**

[b]   That artists will continue to draw our minds upwards into beauty.
Response: **Jesus is Lord.**

[c]   That doctors and surgeons may be caring and skillful.
Response: **Jesus is Lord.**

[d]   That all who preach or teach the Good News may live by it.
Response: **Jesus is Lord.**

[e]   That we would see Jesus in others this day.
Response: **Jesus is Lord.**

[f]   [other prayers]
Response: **Jesus is Lord.**

[g]   Our Father [perhaps sung]

10 Thought-word-phrase for the day

The story of Jesus is Good News

11 Blessing   *Numbers 6:24–26*

May the Lord bless and take care of you.
May the Lord be kind and gracious to you.
May the Lord look on you with favour and give you peace.
     Amen.

12 Concluding music or song

CFE		O&N
246	He is Lord	-
-	Our God sent his Son long ago	435
268	How lovely on the mountains	224

St Simon and St Jude

1 Entrance music (tape or CD) Choose a suitable piece of music

2 Introduction

St. Simon and St. Jude are celebrated on the same day in the Church of the West, but St. Jude has his own feast in the Churches of the East, 19 June. Jesus chose them both as apostles, that is to be his special companions and missionaries. Traditionally both are said to have been martyred in Persia, modern Iran.

Little is known about about Simon except that he was born in Cana. He was known as the "Zealot," which meant that before his conversion to the Gospel he was probably a terrorist opposing Roman occupation.

Jude, also known as Thaddeus, was the apostle who asked Jesus at the Last Supper why he showed himself only to a restricted number of people: only the apostles knew the inner mystery of Jesus (see John 14:22). For a long while there was little devotion to Jude, and people confused him with the traitor of similar name, Judas Iscariot, who betrayed Jesus.

St. Simon is invoked as the Patron of Tanners, whilst St. Jude is invoked as the Patron of Hopeless Cases.

3 Focus or symbol

- One of the shortest books of the New Testament is the Letter of Jude. A focus could be either the Bible opened at the Letter of Jude, or overhead with the whole or part of the letter.

- A box for intentions is placed near a lighted candle.

4 Sign of the Cross

These saints were witnesses to the death and resurrection of Jesus and so we begin, "In the name of the Father and of the Son and of the Holy Spirit."

5 Hymn or song

	CFE		O&N
	175	Follow me, follow me	145

6 Reading   *Extracts from the New Testament Letter of Jude*

May mercy, peace and love be yours in full measure… Fight on for the faith which once and for all God has given to his people… Keep on building yourselves up on your most sacred faith… Pray in the power of the Holy Spirit… Keep yourselves in the love of God as you wait for Our Lord Jesus Christ… Show mercy to those who have doubts.

7 Comment on reading

The traditional prayer to St. Jude reminds us that when we honour the saints or ask for their help, we should try to be better followers of Jesus.

Prayer to St. Jude

St. Jude, glorious apostle, faithful servant and friend of Jesus, the name of the Traitor has caused you to be forgotten by many, but the true Church honours and invokes you as the patron of Hopeless Cases. Pray for me in my need. Make use of that privilege you have been given by God to bring visible and speedy help where it is hard to keep hoping… I promise to be grateful and tell others about the power of Jesus and of the help you give to those who pray to you.

8 Response to reading

Teachers are given a verse of the letter of Jude to tell the pupils about today.

Pupils are invited to place in a box the names of anybody they want to pray for, or some need that they feel strongly about. These papers are burned during the final hymn.

9 Prayers

Loving God hear these prayers which we make through the intercession of St. Simon and St. Jude.

[a]   That the pope, bishops and priests may lead the Church well.

Response: **Lord bless your people.**

[b]   That the work of missionaries may be blessed.

Response: **Lord bless your people.**

[c]   That those who feel hopeless may be helped.

Response: **Lord bless your people.**

[d]   That those who engage in violence or terrorism may turn to peace and gentleness.

Response: **Lord bless your people.**

[e]   That we will all love Jesus more.

Response: **Lord bless your people.**

[f]   [other prayers]

Response: **Lord bless your people.**

[g]   Our Father [perhaps sung]

10 Thought-word-phrase for the day

How can I please Jesus today?

11 Blessing

Jude, v.2

May mercy, peace and love be yours. Amen.

12 Concluding music or song

CFE		O&N
80	Bind us together	-
567	O Lord all the world belongs to you	-
or		
-	For you are my God	152
or		
YOC		
159	We are the Church	-

All Saints

1 Entrance music (tape or CD) Choose a suitable piece of music.

2 Introduction

Today we celebrate the feast of All Saints, in older English All Hallows from which we have Halloween (the evening or eve of All Saints). The saints we think about today include not only all canonised or well-known saints, but also all who are praising God in heaven. These include members of our own family and friends whom we have loved.

3 Focus

- Bible open at beatitudes, or overhead with beatitudes.
- Picture of crowd scene (street, group photo, spectators at sporting event.)

4 Sign of the Cross

The Way of the Cross is the way of love, lived by all the saints, and so we begin "In the name of the Father and of the Son and of the Holy Spirit."

5 Hymn or song

CFE		YOC
187	From heaven you came (The Servant King)	87

CFE		O&N
176	For all the saints	146

 ## 6 Reading   *Matthew 5:1–5*
(paraphrased)

The Beatitudes are Jesus' special teaching showing us genuine values. He said:
- *Happy are those who are poor in spirit –*
  God will give them the Kingdom.
- *Happy are those who mourn –*
  God will comfort them.
- *Happy are those who are gentle –*
  God will give them what he promised.
- *Happy are those who really desire to do what God wants –*
  God will satisfy them fully.
- *Happy are those who are merciful to others –*
  God will be merciful to them.
- *Happy are the pure in heart –*
  God will show himself to them.
- *Happy are those who work for peace –*
  God will; call them his children.
- *Happy are those who suffer because they do what God wants –*
  God will give them the Kingdom.

7 Comment on reading

We all have our heroes, people we admire, or would like to imitate. Those who achieve much in sport and music have to train and practice a lot. The saints had their own training which is the beatitudes, the special way that Jesus taught. If we all tried to be like that, there would be much less pain in the world. Imagine if everyone was modest in spirit, sorry for all evils, gentle, doing what God wants, merciful, working for peace! That is a better way than so much of the hatred, violence, war and crime that we see on TV. The saints put God and others first in their lives, and so they made a huge contribution to the society in which they lived. Yes, it would be nice to be a sporting hero or a great musician, but the world would be a better place if we were all saints in the little things of life.

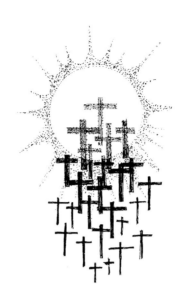

8 Response to reading

Is there some saint that I think is particularly nice? What would I have to do to be more like my patron or favourite saint? Quietly say a little prayer to some saint or to somebody good who has died.

9 Prayers

God of all peoples, we pray with your saints.

[a] That the lives of the saints may spur others to follow Christ.
Response: **Saints of God, come to our help.**

[b] That the courage of the saints may strengthen others who are suffering.
Response: **Saints of God, come to our help.**

[c] That the prayers of the saints may help priests to be holy and dedicated.
Response: **Saints of God, come to our help.**

[d] That the Church may learn from the saints how to walk with the poor.
Response: **Saints of God, come to our help.**

[e] That we may look at the saints in order to know how to live.
Response: **Saints of God, come to our help.**

[f] [other prayers]
Response: **Saints of God, come to our help.**

[g] Our Father [perhaps sung]

10 Thought-word-phrase for the day

The saints are our special friends in heaven

11 Blessing   *Numbers 6:24–26*

May the Lord bless and take care of you.
May the Lord be kind and gracious to you.
May the Lord look on you with favour and give you peace.
    Amen.

12 Concluding music or song

CFE		O&N
571	O when the saints go marching in	437

111

St Margaret of Scotland

1 Entrance music (tape or CD) Choose a suitable piece of music

2 Introduction

Margaret was born in 1046. She was Queen of Scotland. Indeed some branches of our Royal Family can trace their roots back to her, and so to pre-Norman Conquest times. She was very much concerned with reform of the Church in Scotland. She had a great love of scripture. She had eight children. She is buried in Dunfermline alongside her husband, King Malcolm III of Scotland. At the time of the Reformation their bodies were removed to Spain. She is a patron of Scotland alongside St. Andrew.

3 Focus or symbol

- Map of Scotland and/or signs of Scottish culture e.g. tartan, page of music, thistle etc.

4 Sign of the Cross

We begin invoking the Holy Trinity, "In the name of the Father and of the Son and of the Holy Spirit. Amen."

5 Hymn or song

CFE		O&N
288	I watch the sunrise	262

6 Reading   *Proverbs 31:10–14,20*

How hard it is to find a capable wife. She is worth more than jewels!
Her husband puts his confidence in her, and he will never be poor. As long as she lives, she does him good and never harm.
She keeps herself busy; she brings home fine food from out-of-the-way places.
She is generous to the poor and needy.

7 Comment on reading

Margaret lived a very busy life. She was queen and wife, she was mother of eight. She looked after all the affairs of the court; she loved to find time for prayer and for reading the Gospels. Her book of the Gospels is in the Bodleian Library in Oxford. We can learn from her that what God wants is just to do well whatever comes our way. Margaret was good and kind in everything she did: for noble people, for the poor, for her own family. She was a well-rounded saint.

8 Response to reading

We think in silence about our own mums and what we owe them. Is there one nice thing I could do for her, or say to her today?

9 Prayers

We pray for families.

[a]	For the families of all the children and teachers in this school.
Response:	**Teach us to be loving, kind and generous.**
[b]	For those families in the parish who find things difficult at this moment, for those who are lonely and cut off from family members.
Response:	**Teach us to be loving, kind and generous.**
[c]	For the government and parliament that they may support family values.
Response:	**Teach us to be loving, kind and generous.**
[d]	For organisations and people who work for families, for social workers and those in caring professions.
Response:	**Teach us to be loving, kind and generous.**
[e]	For the people of Scotland that they may share the values of their patron, Queen St. Margaret.
Response:	**Teach us to be loving, kind and generous.**
[f]	[other prayers]
Response:	**Teach us to be loving, kind and generous.**
[g]	Our Father [perhaps sung]

10 Thought-Word-Phrase for the day

Thank God for good things we have received from our mum

11 Blessing

The Lord bless us and keep us from all evil, and lead us to everlasting life.
    Amen.

12 Concluding song or music

CFE		*O&N*
347	Lay your hand gently upon us	295

The Presentation of the Blessed Virgin Mary

1 Entrance music (tape or CD) Choose a suitable piece of music

2 Introduction

The Church has always had a deep sense of Mary's holiness. In the Western Church we have the feast of the Immaculate Conception. In the East people thought of Mary as being presented to God in the Temple by her parents Joachim and Anne. The key of this feast is that we celebrate the fact that Mary always belonged to God. Since it is one of the very big feasts in the Churches of the East in places like Greece, Bosnia, Yugoslavia, Russia, we can celebrate with them and remember how much we owe Eastern Christians.

3 Focus of symbol

- An icon, painting, poster, statue or other symbol of Mary.

- Some burning incense as a symbol of prayer going up to heaven.

4 Sign of the Cross

Mary believed, hoped and trusted in God's promises even as her Son was dying on the Cross, and so we begin, "In the name of the Father and of the Son and of the Holy Spirit."

5 Hymn or song

CFE		O&N
S2	As I kneel before you (*Supplement*)	45

 6 Reading *From the liturgy of the Eastern Church (paraphrased)*

The Church of the East thinks of Mary being offered to, and belonging wholly to God and it invites us to think of the scene at the temple.

"O faithful people let us exchange joyful news today, singing psalms to the Lord and hymns of praise in honour of Mary his Mother, his Holy Tabernacle. She is offered to God in a marvellous way, and Zachary, the High Priest, receives her with great joy, for in her God dwells. Today the living temple of God, Mary, the pure and blessed one, is presented in God's temple to live there. Her parents, Joachim and Anne, rejoice with her in the Spirit and all sing praise to their daughter, Mary, who would be one day, Mother of God."

7 Comment on reading

As we think of Mary's being presented in the temple, a symbol that she belonged to God, we think of God's plan for her: she was one day to become the Mother of God. We too belong to God through Holy Baptism, and God has plans for us too, right throughout our lives. We do not have to wait for God's plan: it is always today that he wants us to be good. In fact the Bible gives as Mary's last words to us, "Do whatever he tells you" (John 2:5).

8 Response to reading

Ask for pupils to say, and then write on overhead ways in which we show the beauty of our baptism in our lives; how we are to live according to God's plan for us today.

9 Prayers

On this the Presentation of Mary we offer prayers to God.

[a]	For the parents of children preparing for baptism.
Response:	**Do whatever he tells you.**

[b]	For the Churches of the Christian East.
Response:	**Do whatever he tells you.**

[c]	For the rights of children throughout the world.
Response:	**Do whatever he tells you.**

[d]	For peace and justice in Mary's homeland.
Response:	**Do whatever he tells you.**

[e]	For the grace to live our baptism.
Response:	**Do whatever he tells you.**

[f]	[other prayers]
Response:	**Do whatever he tells you.**

[g]	Our Father [perhaps sung]

10 Thought-word-phrase for the day

I belong to God

11 Blessing   *2 Corinthians 13:13*

The grace of our Lord Jesus Christ, the love of God and the fellowship of the Holy Spirit be with us all.
    Amen.

12 Concluding music or song

CFE		O&N
51	As we come before you now	-
or		
-	O Mary, gentle one	406

St Cecilia

1 Entrance music (tape or CD) Choose a suitable piece of music

2 Introduction

St. Cecilia lived in Rome about the 3rd century. There is very little known about her life. She was martyred because she refused to break a vow she made to God. From the 16th century she has been invoked as the Patron of Music. Today we pray for all musicians.

3 Focus

- A musical instrument and/or a page of music

4 Sign of the Cross

The great sign of the Christian faith is the Cross. So we begin "In the name of the Father and of the Son and of the Holy Spirit."

5 Hymn or song

CFE		O&N
644/645	Sing a new song unto the Lord	480
or		
-	Sing a simple song unto the Lord	481
or		
657	Sing to the Mountains	495

 ## 6 Reading *Psalm 150*

Praise the Lord!
Praise God in his temple
Praise his strength in heaven.
Praise him with trumpets.
Praise him with harps and lyres.
Praise him with drums and dancing.
Praise him with harps and flutes.
Praise him with cymbals.
Praise him with loud cymbals.
Praise the Lord, all living creatures.
Praise the Lord.

7 Comment

In the Old Testament God's people praised him with music and dance. Christians too praise God with hymns. It is good to sing in worship. St. Augustine said, "the one who sings prays twice." But music has a big role in all our lives, but there is a great variety of tastes: folk music, rock, jazz, classical music, the music of various peoples like Africa, Asia, Caribbean etc. Today we give thanks for the gift of music and pray for those who lighten our lives with their gifts.

8 Response to reading

CFE		O&N
-	-	447

(can be sung):

"Praise God from whom all blessings flow,
Praise him all creatures here below.
Praise him above you heavenly host,
Praise Father, Son and Holy Ghost."

9 Let us pray

We give thanks and we pray for musicians.

[a]   We want to appreciate the music of creation.
Response: **Lord you are the music of life.**

[b]   We praise you in music and song.
Response: **Lord you are the music of life.**

[c]   We give thanks for the gift of music.
Response: **Lord you are the music of life.**

[d]   We pray for all who bring music to our lives.
Response: **Lord you are the music of life.**

[e]   We pray for our favourite musicians.
Response: **Lord you are the music of life.**

[f]   We pray for all music teachers and those who encourage the musical gifts of others.
Response: **Lord you are the music of life.**

[g]   [other prayers]
Response: **Lord you are the music of life.**

[h]   Our Father [perhaps sung]

10 Thought-word-phrase for the day

When we enjoy music, we should be considerate of others too, who may not like our music when played too loud.

11 Blessing

May our hearts sing your praises this day and always
     Amen.

12 Concluding music or song

Choose one of the songs that begins with the word "Sing".

CFE		O&N
644–658	Sing...	478–495

117

St Andrew

1 Entrance music (tape or CD) Choose a suitable piece of music

2 Introduction

St. Andrew and his brother St. Peter were fishermen, who were given a new task by Jesus, to become fishers of people. Both were members of the Twelve Apostles and were very close to Jesus. After the resurrection he was a missioner and was put to death as a martyr on an **X**-shaped cross.

His relics were said to have been held in Scotland during the early Middle Ages at a place afterwards called St. Andrew's. He is Patron of that country as well as of Russia. The flag of Scotland carries the X-shaped Cross (St Andrew's Cross), as does the Union Flag of the United Kingdom.

3 Focus or symbol

- Symbols of Scotland, especially a St. Andrew's Cross, **X**,

  or

- Symbols of fishing

4 Sign of the Cross

Legend has it that Andrew did not think he was worthy to be crucified in the same way as Jesus, so he asked for his cross to be sideways. We begin, "In the name of the Father and of the Son and of the Holy Spirit."

5 Hymn or song

CFE		O&N
232	Great St Andrew	-
or		
-	When Christ our Lord to Andrew cried	607

6 Reading
Matthew 4:18–22 (paraphrased)

As Jesus walked along the shore of the Lake of Galilee he saw two brothers, who were fishermen, Simon (called Peter) and his brother Andrew, catching fish in the lake with a net. Jesus said to them, "Come with me and I will teach you to catch people." At once they left their nets and went with him. He then chose the other ten apostles.

7 Comment on reading

Jesus went in search of disciples. He chose them, not they him. Jesus called them in their ordinary daily work. They were fishermen, not educated people, though they were successful enough to own their own boats. Soon they would be taught by Jesus himself, and later by the Holy Spirit.

8 Response to reading

Ask pupils what does it mean to follow Jesus. Write some answers on an overhead.

9 Prayers

We turn to Jesus who searches for us.

[a]   That the Church in Scotland may be strengthened.
Response: **Lord you search me and you know me.**

[b]   That political leaders may follow the values of Jesus.
Response: **Lord you search me and you know me.**

[c]   That fishermen and all who work at sea may be safe.
Response: **Lord you search me and you know me.**

[d]   That the Royal National Lifeboat Institution may continue its great work for those in danger at sea.
Response: **Lord you search me and you know me.**

[e]   That we will treasure our faith in Jesus.
Response: **Lord you search me and you know me.**

[f]   [other prayers]
Response: **Lord you search me and you know me.**

[g]   Our Father [perhaps sung]

10 Thought-word-phrase for the day

Pride in our own culture and nationality

11 Blessing   *Jude v.2*

May mercy, peace and love be yours today, in full measure.
    Amen.

12 Concluding music or song

CFE		O&N
175	Follow me, follow me	145

Christ the King

1 Entrance music (tape or CD) Choose a suitable piece of music

2 Introduction

On the Last Sunday of the Church year we celebrate the Feast of Christ the King, which as it were sums up the whole cycle of feasts. Jesus is King or Lord. But he came not to dominate, but "to serve and give his life to save us all;" (see Matthew 20:28 and *Catechism of the Catholic Church* arts. 541–556, 2816–2821.

The first creed of the Church was "Jesus is Lord" (1 Cor 12:3; Rom 10:9). That is the meaning of this feast. We know that the kingdom, which he wanted to establish on earth, was one in which we would all be better off. It was:

 - A kingdom of truth and life,
 - A kingdom of holiness and grace,
 - A kingdom of justice, love and peace (see the Mass for feast of Christ the King).

 Whenever we say the *Our Father* we pray "Thy Kingdom come."

3 Focus or symbol

 - Some royal symbol, e.g. crown

 - Crucifix

4 Sign of the Cross

The Cross on which Jesus died carried an inscription, which named the "crime" for which he died. It read "Jesus of Nazareth, King of the Jews." And as followers of this great King we begin "In the name of the Father and of the Son and of the Holy Spirit."

5 Hymn or song

CFE		YOC
187	From heaven you came (The Servant King)	87
or		
110	Christ is our King	84

6 Reading　　　*John 18:33-37*

(paraphrased)

Pilate went back into the palace and called Jesus. "Are you the King of the Jews?" he asked him. Jesus answered, "Is this your own question or have you been listening to others?" Jesus said, "My kingdom does not belong to this world." So Pilate asked him "Are you a King then?" Jesus answered, "You say I am a King. I was born and came into the world for this one purpose, to speak about the truth."

7 Comment on reading

The Kingdom of Jesus is not about power or great show. We enter it through baptism and we are to live according to its marks: truth, and life, holiness and grace, justice, love and truth. We build up Christ's Kingdom by our acts of caring and loving, especially when we see people in need.

King of Glory
King of Peace

8 Response to reading

Seven pages or captions are carried in procession carrying the marks of the Kingdom above: truth, life, holiness, grace, justice, love and peace. As these are carried all profess the kingship of Jesus singing "He is Lord" (O&N 206).

9 Prayers

We pray to Christ our King who reigns over heaven and earth.

[a]   For world leaders that they may work for peace.
Response: **Jesus is Lord.**

[b]   For military leaders that they may do what is right.
Response: **Jesus is Lord.**

[c]   For business leaders that they may consider people before profit.
Response: **Jesus is Lord.**

[d]   For Church leaders that they may learn always to serve.
Response: **Jesus is Lord.**

[e]   For ourselves that we may mean what we say, "Thy Kingdom come."
Response: **Jesus is Lord.**

[f]   [other prayers]
Response: **Jesus is Lord.**

[g]   Our Father [perhaps sung]

10 Thought-word-phrase for the day

Jesus is Lord

11 Blessing

May Jesus be Lord of our hearts.
May Jesus be Lord of our homes.
May Jesus be Lord of our school and of our world today.
    Amen.

12 Concluding music or song

CFE		O&N
698	The King of glory comes	527
268	How lovely on the mountains (Our God reigns)	224

St Francis Xavier

1 Entrance music (tape or CD) Choose a suitable piece of music

2 Introduction

Francis was a Basque Spaniard who was born at the castle of Xavier in 1506. He met Ignatius Loyola, the founder of the Jesuit Order at the University of Paris and became fired with a desire to go abroad to preach Christ. He was one of the greatest missionaries of all time. He preached in India, Sri Lanka, the Malay Peninsula and eventually Japan. He died in 1581.

3 Focus or symbol

- A map of Asia/world or globe, and a Cross

4 Sign of the Cross

Francis loved to teach children prayers wherever he went, especially the Our Father, the Hail Mary and the Sign of the Cross. We begin, "In the name of the Father, and of the Son and of the Holy Spirit."

5 Hymn or song

CFE		O&N
268	How lovely on the mountains (Our God reigns)	223/224

6 Reading   *Matthew 28:16–20*

The eleven disciples were on the hill of Galilee where Jesus told them to go. When they saw him, they worshipped him, even though some of them doubted. Jesus drew near and said to them. "I have been given all authority in heaven and on earth. Go, then, to all peoples everywhere and make them my disciples; baptise them in the name of the Father, the Son, and the Holy Spirit, and teach them to obey everything I have commanded you.
And I will be with you always, to the end of the age."

7 Comment on reading

The Church is sent everywhere to share with people the good news about Jesus Christ. Some people feel called to go abroad to bring this message. But we must all be concerned about spreading the Gospel. Wherever we are we must represent Christ and live according to his way. This we do by being truthful, kind, generous, peace loving and by prayer.

8 Response to reading

Invite a pupil/pupils to point out places where Francis preached. Then a poster from some charity supported by the school is held up by a pupil for all to see.

9 Prayers

We pray for the Church throughout the world, and for our role in sharing the good news.

[a]   Bless all those who preach the gospel to others.
Response: **Bring the good news to all.**

[b]   Bless those who suffer for their faith.
Response: **Bring the good news to all.**

[c]   Bless the people of India, Sri Lanka, Malaysia and Japan, where Francis preached.
Response: **Bring the good news to all.**

[d]   Bless us Lord that we may bring good news to others.
Response: **Bring the good news to all.**

[e]   Bless all who serve in our parish.
Response: **Bring the good news to all.**

[f]   [other prayers]
Response: **Bring the good news to all.**

[g]   Our Father [perhaps sung]

10 Thought-Word-Phrase for the day

How can I bring Jesus to others today?

11 Blessing/Prayer

Lord, bless and strengthen each one of us this day and always. Amen.

12 Concluding song or music

CFE		O&N
285	I, the Lord of sea and sky	712

St Nicholas

1 Entrance music (tape or CD) Choose a suitable piece of music

2 Introduction

St. Nicholas was a 4th century bishop of Myra (in present-day Turkey). Very little is known about him, though there was great devotion to him in the Churches of the East and West. Many Churches were dedicated to him.

Legends about him stress his caring and mercy. He was said to have saved three girls by throwing a dowry through their window, as well as many other good deeds. In German speaking areas the custom arose of giving children gifts on his feast day – a custom we have transferred to Christmas time.

He was invoked in times of danger. Indeed in several countries sailors wish one another a safe voyage by saying "May St. Nicholas hold the tiller," that is, "May St. Nicholas steer your boat."

St. Nicholas is invoked as the Patron of children, brides and sailors.

3 Focus or symbol

- Wrapped gift
- Depending on the school it might be appropriate to have a Santa Claus figure, as this name comes via America from an Old Dutch form of St. Nicholas, *Sint Klaas*

4 Sign of the Cross

Generosity is a mark of St. Nicholas. The most generous gift ever was Jesus' death for us on the Cross, and so we begin, "In the name of the Father and of the Son and of the Holy Spirit."

5 Hymn or song

6 Reading

2 Corinthians 9:11–12, 15
(paraphrased)

God will always make you rich enough to be generous at all times, so that others may thank God for the gift they receive from him through us. Gifts serve God's people, and leads to thanksgiving to God. Let us, too, be grateful to God.

7 Comment on reading

People always like to be thanked – we think of somebody who is not grateful as mean-minded. We should always be grateful for the many gifts we receive from God and others. We should always thank our mother or whoever prepares our meals; we should thank God for the beauty of his works.

CFE		O&N
832	You who dwell in the shelter of the Lord	783

8 Response to reading

Sometimes we cannot afford to give gifts or presents to others. But we are never so poor that we cannot offer the gift of kindness. We can play with somebody lonely, we can praise somebody, we can thank a teacher, a parent, and we can be polite in shops, on the bus. Each kind act is a gift.

A short silence for each one to think of a gift to give.

9 Prayers

God is generous and listens to our prayers.

[a]	That the Church and all its members may be more generous.
Response:	**Open our hearts, O Lord.**

[b]	That all children may know kindness and caring.
Response:	**Open our hearts, O Lord.**

[c]	That the Society of St. Vincent de Paul and other charities may be generously supported at Christmas.
Response:	**Open our hearts, O Lord.**

[d]	That the richer countries may have greater concern for the poor of the world.
Response:	**Open our hearts, O Lord.**

[e]	That we may be generous in speech and action.
Response:	**Open our hearts, O Lord.**

[f]	[other prayers]
Response:	**Open our hearts, O Lord.**

[g]	Our Father [perhaps sung]

10 Thought-word-phrase for the day

To show the gift of kindness today

11 Blessing   *Jude v.2*

May mercy, peace and love be yours today, in full measure.
Amen.

12 Concluding music or song

CFE		O&N
662	Sons of God	-
-	Our God sent his Son long ago	435

Immaculate Conception of the Virgin Mary

1 Entrance music (tape or CD) Choose a suitable piece of music

2 Introduction

God had planned from eternity how we were to be saved. The Son was to come to us as man and die for sin. Because the Son was God, all holy and all-pure, the Blessed Trinity wanted to have a very holy mother for him. This mother was Mary. God prepared Mary to be The Mother of God by keeping her free from all sin, even original sin. This is the meaning of saying that she was immaculately conceived: from the first moment of her being she was filled with grace. It seems to have been in England that the feast of the Immaculate Conception was first celebrated about the year 1100.

3 Focus or symbol

– Image of Mary (poster, overhead, statue, icon)

4 Sign of the Cross

Today's feast celebrates the way in which Mary met the salvation of Jesus. We embrace this same gift by saying "In the name of the Father, and of the Son and of the Holy Spirit."

5 Hymn or song

CFE		O&N
300	Immaculate Mary	241
or		
263	Holy Virgin by God's decree	218

6 Reading
Luke 1:26–30 (paraphrased)

In the sixth month of Elizabeth's pregnancy God sent the angel Gabriel to a town in Galilee named Nazareth. He had a message for a girl, whose name was Mary. The angel came to her and said, "Hail favoured one! The Lord is with you. She was very surprised and disturbed by this greeting, wondering what it meant. The angel said to her, "Do not be afraid, Mary, God has specially blessed you."

7 Comment on Reading

We know the great blessings that Mary received in being prepared to be the Mother of God. God wants to bless all of us, and he especially wants to set us free from sin, so that we would be good people, who love God and who do good to others.

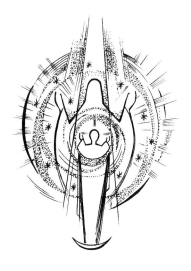

8 Response to reading

We celebrate God's gift to Mary by saying together, "Hail Mary, full of grace…"

9 Prayers

Though we may be sinners and weak, God wants us to draw near to him in prayer.

[a]	For the Church: that like Mary it may be holy and good.
Response:	**Holy Mary, pray for us.**

[b]	For the world: that sin and injustice may give way to peace and love.
Response:	**Holy Mary, pray for us.**

[c]	For ourselves: that we may try to be good.
Response:	**Holy Mary, pray for us.**

[d]	For those in trouble: that they may find help and strength.
Response:	**Holy Mary, pray for us.**

[e]	For England: that it may once more be the Dowry of Mary.
Response:	**Holy Mary, pray for us.**

[f]	[other prayers]
Response:	**Holy Mary, pray for us.**

[g]	Our Father [perhaps sung]

10 Thought-Word-Phrase for the day

*"O Mary,
conceived without sin,
pray for us who have
recourse to you."*

11 Blessing/prayer

Jesus, the Author of Life, came to us through Mary, may we always rejoice in her loving care.

12 Concluding song or music

CFE		O&N
476	Maiden yet a mother	-
538	O Lady, full of God's own grace	-
561	Of one that is so fair and bright	-
652	Sing of Mary, pure and lowly	-
-	Mary most holy	347
-	O Mary gentle one	406

The lives of saints used to have many fictional or legendary details made up to edify. But what is not true will rarely be helpful in the long run. Since the 17th century there has been a great deal of emphasis on accurate lives of the saints. Two dictionaries can be strongly recommended:

- THE OXFORD DICTIONARY OF SAINTS, 4th edition (1997), David Farmer.

- PENGUIN DICTIONARY OF SAINTS 3rd edition (1995) D. Attwater and his daughter.

- The classic, BUTLER'S LIVES OF THE SAINTS, can be found in many editions, reprints and abbreviations.

- Useful too are books such as ONE HUNDRED SAINTS: THEIR LIVES AND LIKENESS (Boston–London: Bullfinch Press, Little, Brown and Company, 1993) often remaindered. Such books are very suitable for libraries.

- SAINTS OF THE DAY: LIVES AND LESSONS FOR SAINTS AND FEASTS OF THE NEW MISSAL (Cincinnati: St Anthony Messenger, 1990) L.Foley

There are many helpful books of prayers of, or to, the saints, such as:

- THE SAINTS PRAYER BOOKS (Norwich: Canterbury Press, 1998). A.F. Chiffolo.

- THE CATHOLIC PRAYERBOOK FROM DOWNSIDE ABBEY (Edinburgh: Clark, 1999). D. Foster, ed.

Available from McCrimmons

Clip art on CD:

- SIGNS, SYMBOLS & SAINTS – VOL.1 600+ high quality black & white images on CD. Ref: SSSCD

- SIGNS, SYMBOLS & SAINTS – VOL.2 280+ high quality colour images taken from vol.1. Ref: SSSCD2

The Rainbow Story series for children:

- SAINT FRANCIS OF ASSISI Dorothy Smith ISBN 0 85597 394 3

- SAINT JOAN OF ARC Dorothy Smith ISBN 0 85597 414 1

- THERESE, THE LITTLE FLOWER OF LISIEUX Dorothy Smith ISBN 0 85597 3994

- THOMAS MORE THE KING'S GOOD SERVANT Dorothy Smith ISBN 0 85597 431 1